The ancient Borough
of Newport in Pembrokeshire -

Dillwyn Miles
ISBN - 0-860 750949.

A BOOK ON NEVERN

Dillwyn Miles

First Impression—1998

ISBN 1 85902 578 1

Printed in Wales by
Gomer Press, Llandysul, Ceredigion, Wales.

CONTENTS

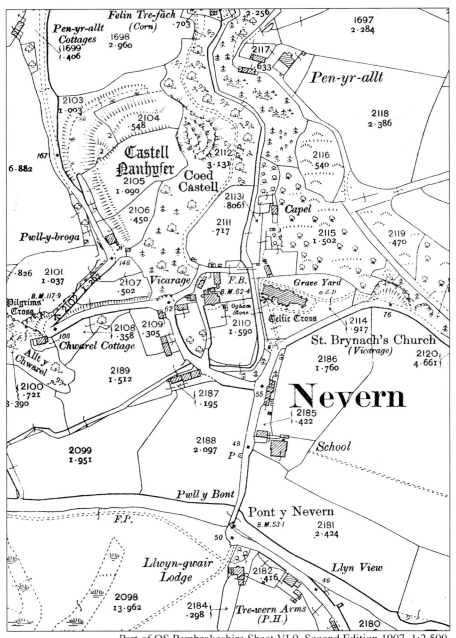

Part of OS Pembrokeshire Sheet VI.9, Second Edition 1907, 1:2,500.

ILLUSTRATIONS

ACKNOWLEDGEMENTS

When I begin to think of those to whom I owe a debt for their help in writing this little book, I should include my grandmother, though dead for sixty years, who told me about the way she used to avoid the Welsh-Not at Nevern School, and play five-stones sitting on the wedge-shaped cutwater on Nevern Bridge, and straddle a horse from the mounting-block by the church gate, and Aunt Bess, who spoke about the tenants of the churchyard and was buried among them, but only by sharing her parents' grave: at 102 she had waited too long. Then there was my father who took me, as a small boy, on the long walk, past the round Lodge and Llwyngwair stables, under tall holm oaks and through Sandy Lane, to see his friend the vicar, Lewis Roderick, at the vicarage. I should also thank the parishioners who, fifty years ago, elected me their County Councillor and thus enabled me to get to know every corner of the parish, one of the largest in Wales, and its people intimately.

I am grateful to the Very Reverend Bertie Lewis, formerly Dean of St David's, who was Vicar of Nevern and with whom I discussed the idea of writing the book; Mr Penry Evans, Clerk of the Parish Council for many years and the possessor of a vast store of inherited information to which he has added during his active lifetime; the Dean of St David's (The Very Reverend Wynn Evans); Stephen Watkins, JP, of Trewern; John Burgess of Birmingham; Harold Davies of Eglwyswrw, and Martin Lewis of Newport, each of whom contributed to the fund of gathered knowledge. To Anthony and Di, who made a photographying expedition enjoyable, and to Dr Dyfed Elis-Gruffydd of Gomer Press who took such care with the publication of the book, I wish to extend my grateful thanks. And, of course, to Judith, not only for putting up with me, but also for tape-recording epitaphs in a manner that makes it a pleasure to listen to an instant remembrance of departed souls.

DILLWYN MILES

Nevern Bridge, the old school and schoolhouse, and the church.

INTRODUCTION

In seeking to portray the hamlet of Nevern, one soon runs out of superlatives, for there are few places where beauty, tranquillity and sanctity dwell more softly, or in greater measure.

I first wrote about Nevern in a Welsh poem, a sonnet, when I was a lad, mad with love for her of the flaxen hair and sky blue eyes whom I had brought to share my Elysium. 'Beneath the canopy of yews, dark sentinels, each in its leafy livery, apart from the wounded one, bleeding for ever, we walked towards the church, hand in hand; and when we climbed to the rock-cut cross, she knelt and said: "One little one, for us both, that we should never part".' So the sonnet ran.

I now endeavour, as no one has done so before, to bring together and to place on record some of that which is known about Nevern, in the hope that it will inspire others to dig deeper into its past.

The village lies in a verdant bowl that turns to gold in autumn, save for the yew trees, out of which peeps the squat tower of the church: a few cottages, a vicarage and a school converted into a village hall, and an inn. The lion within an orle of roses on the sign outside the Trewern Arms bespeaks a people that were old when the Normans seized their stronghold on the hill opposite.

I am aware that I have struck an imbalance in writing of remembered people. John Jones (Tegid) receives more space not only on account of his stature but also because so little has been written about him elsewhere. George Owen of Henllys, the greatest of them all, has had short shrift as he has been so well documented by Dr B G Charles in his *George Owen of Henllys: A Welsh Elizabethan* and, in a more modest way, in the introduction to my edition of his *Description of Pembrokeshire*.

I have included, as a final chapter, under the heading *Nevern 1600*, a modernised version of George Owen's 'Second Book' insofar as it referred to the gentry residences within the parish.

View from the
Bridge—
1900 and 1997.

NYFER / NANHYFER / NEVERN

The name Nyfer is old in legend. When Arthur and his knights were hunting *Twrch Trwyth*, a king transformed by God for his sins into a fierce wild boar, and pursued it over the Presely Hills, 'all the warriors ranged themselves around the Nyver'[1] and then went on 'from Glyn Nyver to Cwm Kerwyn'. The Welsh annals, *Annales Cambriae*, refer to Nant Nyfer, the valley of the Nyfer, as *nant nimer* and record that *Cian nant nimer*, of whom nothing else is known, died in 865 AD. The parish, the church and the village are known to their people as *Plwy'r Nyfer* and *Eglwys y Nyfer* and *Y Nyfer*, taking the name from Afon Nyfer, the river that rises on the slopes of Frenni Fawr and flows in a westerly direction to the sea at Newport. In the Welsh language such a word would develop a final *n*, to give *Nevern*.

Nanhyfer also appears in an eleventh-century poem[2] by Meilyr Brydydd who claimed that he was present at the battle of Mynydd Carn, fought at the end of a day's march northward from St David's, in 1081. He mourns the death of a king of Gwynedd at the hands of Irish mercenaries whom he describes contemptuously, and mysteriously, as

> *pobl anhyfaeth Nanhyfer*
> *Gwyddyl diefyl duon.*

(the intractable people of Nanhyfer, Irish black devils).

No one has been able to interpret his strange words.

Nanhyfer/Nevern sign.

13

Giraldus Cambrensis,[3] when he passed by on Monday, 28 March 1188, referred to *Llanhyver*, where *llan* was mistakenly substituted for *nant*, and this form appeared from time to time up to the eighteenth century.

The earliest evidence of human activity in north Pembrokeshire was found on the south bank of the Nevern below Newport Bridge. Here people of the Mesolithic Age shaped their microlithic barbs and arrows to fish and to hunt, and a stone tranchet axe, uncovered nearby during recent excavation, was made in about 7000 BC[4] and used to cut down trees. The sea level was considerably lower then, and forested land reached out into Newport Bay, the submerged remains of which are occasionally exposed on Traeth Mawr.

A more widespread settlement occurred with the arrival of the first farmers who brought their stock and seedcorn about 4000 BC. There are no remains of their dwellings nearer than Clegyr Boia, near St David's, but their massive chambered tombs indicate the existence of a community that was in a considerably advanced state of intellectual development.

There are four chambered tombs, or *cromlechi*, in the parish of Nevern. Trellyffant and Llech-y-drybedd stand on the high coastal plain and may have been built by people who moved from the valley to a less heavily wooded area, while Pentre Ifan and Bedd-yr-afanc are the tombs of those who moved up the valley. The different types of tombs suggest that the area was colonized by small groups of people who made landfall from Ireland at different times along the north Pembrokeshire coast.

The tombs were the objects of man's conjecture for centuries. They were believed to be the graves of giants, altars to gods or druids, or the playthings of kings or of the devil. For a long time, King Arthur's Quoit was an alternative name for a *cromlech*, and Llech-y-drybedd was said to be a quoit hurled from the topmost peak of Carn Ingli by Samson, whose grave lay beside the Nevern at Bedd Samson.

Llech-y-drybedd (SN101432), 'the tripod stone', is appropriately named as it has three squat uprights, two of which support a massive capstone. A stone lying prostrate on the ground may be the fourth upright which, Erasmus Saunders informed Edward Lhuyd in 1693,[5] also supported the capstone. There is no evidence of a mound or cairn on the heavily cultivated site. The floor of the chamber lies below the present ground level and the monument would therefore have appeared taller in its original form. The tomb belongs to the portal dolmen tradition of the Irish Sea province, where the front uprights appear as a door to the tomb and the capstone has a thick end over the portal.

Richard Fenton regarded Llech-y-drybedd as 'one of the most perfect of that species of druidical relics called Cromlech we have in the county'[6] and used a drawing of the monument by Sir Richard Colt Hoare as a frontispiece for his book, *A Historical Tour through Pembrokeshire*. Fenton adds that at the west end of the field in which the chamber stands, 'towards the sea, I pass a stone called Maen y tri thivedd, or the stone of the three heirs, the possessions of three men having met there.' The stone is said to be buried in the hedge between the field and the lane, west of the chamber.

Trellyffant (SN082425) is a double-chambered tomb of the portal dolmen kind, consisting of two megalithic structures set side by side, one being much larger than the other. The megaliths are almost certainly selected local erratics. The capstone of the smaller chamber is missing and only three sidestones remain, facing south-west like the larger chamber. The surface of the surviving capstone, which is supported by only two of the four uprights, is covered with 35 cupmarks, a form of decoration for which there is no satisfactory explanation.

Pentre Ifan (SN099370) is one of the most impressive megalithic monuments in the country. George Owen of Henllys, writing in 1603, thought it worth noting 'the stone called Maen y gromlech upon Pentre Ifan land' and went on to describe it as 'a huge and massive stone mounted on high and set on the tops of three other high stones pitched standing upright in the ground. It far surpasses for bigness and height . . . any other that I ever saw, saving some in Stonehenge . . . The stones whereon this is laid are so high that a man on horseback may well ride under it without stooping.' He made a drawing of the cromlech which is one of the earliest known representations of a megalithic monument.[7]

The chamber stands in a field called Corlan Samson, 'Samson's fold'.

Pentre Ifan cromlech with Carn Ingli in the background.

The high portal and crescentic facade makes the site unique among Welsh megalithic monuments and associates it with the court-cairns of northern Ireland and south-west Scotland. Between the two uprights at the forecourt end is a stone that gives the appearance of a doorway, but it is firmly wedged and is of symbolic value only. In practice, successive internments were introduced at the side of the chamber.

The chamber was excavated by Professor W F Grimes in 1936, and again in 1958. No trace of burial was found and, therefore, it is not known whether cremation or inhumation was practised. A monument of such a size would have been used for burials over a period of time, yet the finds were meagre and comprised a few sherds of round-bottomed pots and some flakes of flint that included a triangular arrowhead.

Professor Grimes observed that 'the structure is cunningly set to face uphill so that the votary, walking towards the entrance during the burial ceremonial, would see beyond the great megaliths nothing but remote vistas.'

Bedd-yr-afanc (SN109346) was excavated in 1939 by Grimes who described it as 'an exceptional site in Wales'. Jacquetta Hawkes considered it to be 'hardly megalithic' because the stones were so small. Its low cairn, like an island in a bog, is orientated east-west and within the cairn is a type of gallery grave which may be influenced by the Irish long cairn tradition. A passage with ten pairs of low uprights leads to a small circular chamber, but no capstone survives. Its name may be translated literally as 'the grave of an aquatic monster'. Local legend has it that the Afanc was caught in a pool below Brynberian Bridge and was dragged 'up the hill, to be buried with pomp and religious rites', by five or six *ychain bannog* (horned oxen).[8]

Standing stones appear to be linked to the religious background of the Bronze Age. They are often situated on the open flanks of valleys, or near streams and, with some exceptions, such as Bedd Morus at Newport, they are not in conspicuous positions, nor can it be said that they have been erected as route markers. Some of the ones that have been excavated were revealed to be associated with burials, and others had evidence of ritual and could have been objects of worship or of fertility rites. They were connected with the Beaker people, although no beakers have been found associated with any of them in Pembrokeshire, and the variety of the situations in which they occur suggests a practice that spread among the indigenous Bronze Age population. A tendency has been noted for the stones to be distributed along the transpeninsular trade route used by the Beaker people travelling to Ireland so as to avoid the perilous headland tides and races.

The standing stones identified in the parish of Nevern are Y Garreg Hir (SN064351) which stands some nine feet high off the road between Gellifawr and Trefach; the Trellyffant Stone (SN083423) standing south of the burial chamber; the Penparcau Stone (SN091354); the Tafarn-y-bwlch Stone (SN081332) on the roadside between Tafarn-y-bwlch and Bwlch Gwynt, and the Waun Mawn Stone (SN080339) which stands on the open moor west of Tafarn-y-bwlch, near a pair of standing stones. They sometimes appear in pairs, where the stones are set side by side with their faces roughly in the same plane. A pair at Parc Lan (SN090358), in contrast to the other six pairs in the county, face each other. One stone in each pair is invariably larger than the other and usually square-topped, while its partner is slighter and frequently tapering at the point. There is also a group of stones of uncertain character on Waun Mawn (SN084340). It has been suggested that there could be a link between the stone pairs of west Wales and the paired stones of West Kennet Avenue at Avebury, each pair consisting of stones that were carefully differentiated in shape and some having Beaker burials at their foot.

A group of Bronze Age barrows on Crugiau Cemais was described by George Owen as 'four little tumps of earth, and yet to be seen forty miles off, viz, from Pumlumon.' Edward Lhuyd, almost a century later, noted four barrows, one of which had recently been dug, when five urns had been found, together with burnt bones and ashes. One of the urns was presented to the Ashmolean Museum, Oxford. Two other mounds were later identified. Fenton stated that this was the largest group of barrows in the county, with the exception of the group at Dry Burrows (SR948997) where there were seven barrows. The Crugiau Cemais barrows had a narrow escape from being destroyed by an inconsiderate landlord in 1951, and were only saved when the bulldozer turned upon its driver and ran over his foot and this enabled me as the local correspondent of the Ancient Monuments Board to obtain a protection order.

Foel Eryr (SN066321) has a round cairn, built of mountain-strewn stones, at its summit, known locally as Carnedd y Lladron (the thieves' cairn). The prospect from the summit embraces the greater

Pair of Standing Stones near Tafarn-y-bwlch.

18

part of the county and beyond to Dunkery Beacon in the south and Snowdonia to the north, on a clear day, and occasionally to the Wicklow Hills: a National Park viewpoint has an observation beacon to interpret the panoramic scene. Foel Feddau (SN103323) has a drystone cairn, overgrown with turf, at the summit, and Mynydd Du (SN079312) has a much disturbed cairn in which white quartz appears in its construction. These cairns lie along, or near, the ancient trackway that follows the ridge of the Presely Hills variously marked on maps as Roman Road, Flemings' Way, and Robbers' Road.

The exploitation of the rocks of Presely begun in Neolithic times continued into the Bronze Age. Axe-hammers and perforated mace-heads were made of spotted ophitic dolerite, the 'bluestone' of the stone pillars conveyed from the Presely Hills to Stonehenge. A pestle-mace of this dolerite, found on Cilgwyn Farm (SN089363) in 1946, provided a rare example of the flattened pestle type of perforated mace-head.

A bronze palstave,[9] without loop, was found in 1924 in a field near Pentre Ifan, and a fragmentary riveted spearhead was unearthed in the vicinity some time afterwards. A halberd[10] found near Pont Brynberian was only the second of its kind to be found in Wales.

Castell Henllys (SN117391)[11] is an inland promontory fort of the Iron Age positioned on a spur overlooking the river Duad. The site has been excavated and the settlement partly recreated in order to give an impression of life as it was lived around two thousand years ago.

The main defences lie on the vulnerable landward side, on each side of the main entrance, and a *chevaux de frise* was erected beyond the defensive banks in order to prevent an attack by cavalry or chariots. The steep sides of the spur were terraced and defended by a pallisaded bank in places. The number of roundhouses traced, together with square or rectangular storage huts or granaries, indicate that the settlement could have accommodated a community of around a hundred souls. There was evidence of iron working and other agricultural activities.

An area to the north of the fort was found to have been used as a farmstead during the early Christian period, after the fort had been abandoned. It revealed imported pottery of various kinds, iron objects, fragments of glass, corroded remains of bronze brooches and a complete quern stone of non-local rock.

Castell Cynon (SN035345), a promontory fort standing above the confluence of a small stream and the river Gwaun, has a well-preserved single bank that provided defence from the west, while the steep slope on the eastern side was sufficient. A panel gives information about the site and the surrounding landscape.

Castell Trefach (SN087409) stands on a spur above the confluence of the river Caman and a tributary.

The site of Nevern Castle may well have been an Iron Age fort, but there is no evidence of this and none is likely to be available without excavation.

When the rest of Britain was occupied by the Romans, Ptolemy states that south-west Wales remained the territory of the Demetae. By the fifth century, an Irish tribe, the Deisi, colonised Pembrokeshire and established a dynasty of Irish kings that was to last until the tenth. They brought with them a script that was known as ogham, from Ogma, its supposed inventor, which they used to inscribe the names of their dead on early Christian monuments. The ogham alphabet had twenty characters, each formed of up to five parallel notches or strokes cut on either side of the arris, or edge, of a stone pillar. The inscription usually bore the name of a man and frequently indicated his paternity by the use of the word *maqi*, the Goidelic for 'son of', corresponding to the Welsh *mab* or *ap* The inscription appears in ogham only in Ireland but in Wales it is often accompanied by the Latin form: the one in Nevern church appears in ogham as *Maglocunas maqi Clutar(i)* and in Latin as *Maglocuni fili Clutori*. The inscriptions date from the fifth, or early sixth, centuries.

Stones inscribed with a cross only belong to the seventh century and pillar stones thus inscribed are to be found at Penparcau (SN092353), now set up in front of the cottage, and at Trehaidd (SN096531) where a stone with a linear cross forms part of a flight of steps in an outbuilding.[12] At Trebwlch farm (SN087352) there are three inscribed pillar stones, one with an incised linear cross, and the other two each having two linear Latin ring-crosses conjoined, one above the other, on a common stem. At Cilgwyn church (SN077359) a cross-incised stone has been built into the corner of the church.

The Pilgrims' Cross (SN081400), situate along a path leading off the road from the village to Nevern Castle, at a hair-pin bend, is a

The Pilgrim's Cross, with kneeling place or place for offerings.

rock-hewn cross cut in relief in the living rock. One historian 'plausibly urged that it lay on the route to St David's from Strata Florida and Holywell',[13] and there was also a belief that Nevern was the last stage of the pilgrimage to the cathedral city and that 'at this point pilgrims often found their strength fail them, and expired, and were buried in the adjoining [sic] churchyard.'[14] A ledge below the cross 'on which devotees knelt and supplicated the saint to prosper their journey' is now considered more likely to have been a place for offerings. The cross is in the ownership of the Representative Body of the Church in Wales and is scheduled as a monument of national importance under the Ancient Monuments and Archaeological Areas Act of 1979.

SAINT BRYNACH

The saint of Nevern is Brynach, who lived in the sixth century. His *Vita*[1] has been described as 'ominously vague'[2]: it does not refer to his parentage, except to say that he originated 'from an illustrious stock of progenitors', and there is no indication as to the land of his birth. His name corresponds to the Irish Bernach and it may be that he was Irish by birth: he has been confused with the legendary Brynach Wyddel.[3] It is also considered that he may have come from the Middle East, as the route of his travels was to Rome, and then to Brittany, and finally to Pembrokeshire. After he had landed on a bank of the river Cleddau, a nobleman's daughter fell madly in love with him and mixed him a drink of wolfsbane as a love potion. He managed to escape but the lady, thwarted in love, hired evil men to ambush him. One of them pierced him with his lance, but Brynach bathed his wound in a nearby spring, making the water run red with blood: the well was known thereafter as *Fons Rubeus*[4] and became a healing well. He then came to the previously uninhabitable valley of the Gwaun at *Pons Lapideus*,[5] Pontfaen, where he subdued evil spirits and founded a church before moving on to *Saltus Veteris Ecclesii*, otherwise Llwyn Henllan. Here he was told: 'This is not the place for thy dwelling. Go along the bank to the second rill, which flows into the river, and watch until you see a white sow with her piglets. There dwell.' And there, on the bank of the Caman, he established his monastery.

The land on which he did so belonged to one Clechre, or Clether, an old man who had twenty sons. He surrendered it voluntarily to Brynach and left his sons as Brynach's disciples, while he retired to Cornwall where he lived a life of devotion at St Clether, near Launceston.[6]

Brynach possessed a cow which he gave into the custody of a wolf which acted as herdsman.[7] Maelgwn, king of Gwynedd, came by one day and demanded that the saint should prepare supper for him and his retinue. When Brynach refused, the king sent his men to seize the cow, which they killed and prepared for cooking, but when the water would not boil, Maelgwn perceived that the Lord had intervened on

23

Brynach's behalf. He and his servants humbled themselves before the saint, and the cow was restored to life and placed in the wolf's custody once more. Brynach invited the king to stay the night and fed him and his men with wheaten bread from an oak tree and wine from the water of the Caman.[8] There are several legends in which Maelgwn Gwynedd came into conflict with a saint and in most cases they are intended to exalt the saint at the expense of the king.[9]

The cow and the wolf are commemorated at Cas-fuwch (Castlebythe) and Cas-blaidd (Wolfscastle), and also at Llanboidy, 'the monastery of the cow-house' and at Buarth Brynach, Brynach's cow-fold.

Another onomastic legend presents Brynach ascending to the summit of Carn Ingli to commune with angels in order to provide a derivation from Carn Engyl, and *Mons angelorum*, 'mount of angels', instead of 'Ingli's cairn'.

Brynach's feast day is the seventh day of April and it was commonly believed that the cuckoo came on that day and sat on Saint Brynach's stone. The priest would not begin mass until the bird had first appeared, according to a legend recorded by George Owen, but one year it was late arriving and when it 'came at last, lighting on the said stone, her accustomed preaching place, and being scarce able once to sound the note, presently fell dead. This vulgar tale,' Owen adds, 'although it concern in some sort church matters, you may either believe or not without peril of damnation.'[10]

There were several wells dedicated to Brynach.[11] Ffynnon Brynach, or Bernard's Well, lying near the old chapel of Saint Brynach in the parish of Henry's Moat,[12] is protected by a modern masonry hood and alongside it are the traces of a well-chamber. Fenton stated that there was 'a rude stone pitched on end near it, rudely marked with a cross.' He had come to the conclusion, however, 'from some curious MS. notes of the great antiquary George Owen' that the principal fountain dedicated to Saint Brynach 'lies above that range of rocks called Cernydd Meibion Owen, on the side of the mountain by the highway, and is compassed round with a curtilage of stone wall called Buarthbrynach, Brynach's Fold', and there the pious saint 'passed his days in austerity and solitude'. Other wells[13] dedicated to him were Ffynnon Brynach at Llanfyrnach, and another at Llanfair Nantgwyn, and Pistyll Brynach spouts on to the beach on Newport Sands.

When Brynach arrived at Nevern, he would have entered an area that was already rich in Christian tradition, as witnessed by the early Christian monuments in the church and churchyard.

Nevern was a traditional Celtic monastic settlement, or *clas*, with its consecrated enclosure, or *llan*, in which the dead were buried and upon which, later, a monastery, and eventually a church, was erected so that, with time, *llan* came to signify a church, frequently having attached to it the name of the missionary, or 'saint', of local reputation to whom the church was dedicated. That some of the 'saints' merited a wider recognition is indicated by the number of dedications to them. The distribution of the cult of Brynach is demonstrated by dedications to him, apart from Nevern, at Llanfyrnach, Pontfaen, Dinas and Henry's Moat in Pembrokeshire, at Llanboidy across the border in Carmarthenshire, at Llanfrynach near Brecon and Llanfrynach in Glamorgan.[14] It has been suggested that the overall distribution of these dedications is similar to that of the ogham-inscribed stones and related to the ancient trackways and Roman roads leading from the Western Seas.

The church at Braunton, near Barnstaple, is dedicated to St Brannoc, who is said to have crossed the sea from Wales. A boss above the font portrays a litter of pigs in reference to a local legend that Brannoc was told in a dream to build his church where he would find a sow suckling her piglets.

The tradition of St Brynach was deep-rooted at Nevern and it survived the Norman disposition to dedicate, or re-dedicate, churches to the Virgin Mary, or one of their favourite saints.

Brynach has been said to have married Corth, or Cymorth, a daughter of Brychan, the eponymous king of Brycheiniog, who does not appear among the twenty-four daughters of the king, but was a fictitious person invented by Iolo Morganwg as the wife of the legendary Brynach Wyddel.[15]

NEVERN CASTLE

The cantref of Cemais was spared the attention of Roger de Montgomery as he marched south to Pembroke in 1093 but, not much more than a decade later, it was invaded by Robert, son of Martin,[1] a tenant-in-chief in the West Country who gave his name to places such as Combe Martin and Compton Martin. He is thought to have been in possession before 1108, when Gerald of Windsor seized Cilgerran and the Flemings settled in Rhos and Daugleddau, having occupied the stronghold of the native ruler at Nevern, where he established his *caput baroniae*.

As heir to vast estates in Devon, Dorset and Somerset and, later, their lord, and in view of his active support of the Empress Matilda, and other commitments, it is not likely that Robert was able to devote much of his time to his newly acquired lordship in Wales. He may well have left it in the charge of a steward or, as is known to have happened elsewhere, the advantages of a peaceful co-existence was realised by both sides and the vanquished ruler may have been left in a position of authority, but under the jurisdiction of the invader.

Nevern, before the arrival of FitzMartin, would appear to have been the stronghold of Cuhelyn, son of Gwynfardd Dyfed whose name suggests that he was a poet of high regard with a reputation extending beyond the boundaries of Cemais, and from whom the leading families of north Pembrokeshire claim descent to the present time. Cuhelyn, too, was a poet of standing and is usually referred to as Cuhelyn Fardd, and a later descendant was the greatest of medieval Welsh poets, Dafydd ap Gwilym. Cuhelyn is eulogised in an obscure poem in *The Black Book of Carmarthen*[2] in which he is ascribed the cardinal virtues of generosity, wisdom and courage and is described as 'a leader of the hosts' and 'a ruler of Britons'. He is also described in the pedigree as *tywysog* (prince).

Nevern was established as a small borough, with a portreeve and its own courts, and there is account that it had eighteen burgages.

In 1136 Robert FitzMartin, along with Stephen, constable of Cardigan, and other Anglo-Normans and Flemings, were routed by the

Welsh at the battle of Crug Mawr, north of Cardigan, and Cemais remained in Welsh hands for the next twenty years.

Robert died in 1159 and was succeeded by his son, William FitzMartin who married Angharad, daughter of Rhys ap Gruffydd, prince of Deheubarth. Soon after Henry II came to the throne, in 1154, Rhys had to submit to the king and restore their former possessions to the Anglo-Normans. Henry, in return, confirmed him in his original territories and appointed him Justiciar, with authority over the subordinate princes. He was known, henceforth, as The Lord Rhys.

Rhys recaptured Cardigan in 1165 and built a castle of stone and mortar there, in which he held the first recorded *eisteddfod* in 1176.

When Henry died in 1189, Rhys and his sons overran south-west Wales and, in 1191, he attacked Nevern castle and drove out his son-in-law, William FitzMartin and gave it to his eldest son, Gruffydd, but by 1194 the castle was in the hands of Gruffydd's envious brother, Maelgwn. In that year, Rhys was in conflict with his sons Maelgwn and Hywel Sais and was imprisoned by them in Nevern castle. He did not remain captive for long, however, as Hywel took the castle from Maelgwn and released his father.

Giraldus Cambrensis, in the account[3] of his journey through Wales with Archbishop Baldwin of Canterbury preaching the Third Crusade, referred to this 'extraordinary event' stating that Rhys had acted 'in direct contravention of a whole series of oaths which he had sworn in person on the most precious relics to the effect that William should be left in all peace and security in his castle,' and when Rhys was imprisoned by his own sons in his own castle, Giraldus reckoned that 'God took vengeance on him in the most apposite way.'

In 1195 Hywel dismantled Nevern castle so as 'to avoid it falling into English hands'[4] and, according to one account, he lost control of Cemais that year.[5] Rhys died in April 1197 and was succeeded by his son Gruffydd.

In 1196 William FitzMartin obtained a loan of 20 marks (£13.33) from the Crown to restore or re-fortify his 'castle of Cemais'.[6] It is thought that he may have regained control of Cemais for a brief period and that the money was used to refurbish Nevern. On the other hand, he was already establishing his new borough at Newport,[7] and Nevern, as a *caput*, was abandoned.

27

The first authoritative report[8] on Nevern castle was provided by Cathcart King and Clifford Perks whom the author took there following a visit they made to Newport castle in the summer of 1949. As the whole area was heavily overgrown, we had to enter a gap in the hedge from the road and climb the steep bank to the bailey. This was extremely difficult for King as he had lost a leg during the war. His notes on the visit gives a succinct description of the site:

> The site is triangular: on the N it is defended by a slight fall in the ground, the W side which slopes to the S is more or less level with the ground in front of it. The hypotenuse, the long, straggling SE side, overhangs the stream; the apex, at the NW, is occupied by the motte. At the eastern angle is a Very Singular Work [VSW]. Along the SE side no special defence was needed; on the W there was a most redoubtable bank and ditch; on the N, two, but with a difference. The motte is the self-sacrificing kind: on the uphill or weak side, with no ditch against its bailey. The bank on the W, and the *outer* bank on the N, both abut against its sides.

The dense growth, mostly blackthorn, made movement difficult and King, though 'excused by lameness from an exhaustive exploration', boasted that he 'was stout Cortez, and first beheld the VSW. It was a thrilling, but horrifying, experience for none of us had hitherto seen anything like it.' He went on to describe it:

> At the projecting point of the bailey, where it ended in a towering Rhenish crag, a deep and wide ditch, with the most beautifully smooth and vertical sides, had been cut in the solid shale, isolating a small level platform . . . The platform still has the remains of a stout wall around it, too much of a stump for description or measurement, and on the W, overlooking the ditch, is a tower.

The report concluded that the site consisted of 'a motte-and-bailey castle out of which a piece had been cut to make a strong stone castle.' This castle was isolated by a deep rock-cut ditch: the other two sides were defended adequately by the cliffs and steep slopes of the Caman gorge. The castle was quite unlike any English castle and it would appear to have been built by The Lord Rhys.

Nevern Castle—the 'Very Singular Work'.

The castle and the surrounding woodland were purchased by the Nevern Community Council in 1980 for the sum of £3,000. The site was cleared and made accessible to the public, for which the Council received a Prince of Wales Award.

The clearance of the site exposed a stone revetment along the north face of the outer bank, together with the remains of a small tower on the motte, which suggested that the original plan had been radically altered. This led Dr Roger Turvey[9] to come to the conclusion that the inner castle had been built at the same time as the alterations to the motte-and-bailey and that the whole of the reconstruction had been carried out by The Lord Rhys after he had evicted FitzMartin.

NEVERN CHURCHYARD

One approaches the church under a canopy of yew trees that have stood there for untold centuries. When a branch was sawn off the second tree on the right, to make way for the digging of a grave some years ago, it was found that a blood-like sap oozed from the exposed pith, and people come in thousands, each year, to view the phenomenon of 'the Bleeding Yew'. No one has been able to offer an acceptable explanation for this rare, if not unique, occurrence. Among the leading arboricultural authorities, one says that it might be 'sap from a fungal-infected wound',[1] while another believes that 'the red exudation reflects breakdown of the heartwood of the tree'.[2] Yet another considers the possibility of rainwater 'becoming trapped in the reddish heart of the gashed yew and emerging coloured'[3] and adds that 'a reddish plasma resembling blood is unusual'. Legends soon burgeoned, however: a man, or was it not a monk, was hanged from this branch, for stealing the church plate, or for some infringement of the forest law, and the unfortunate's last words were that the tree would bleed for ever to proclaim his guiltlessness. A more political version states that it will weep blood until a Welshman occupies Nevern castle again.

The yew tree had significance in pre-Christian times.[4] It was credited with magical properties: magic wands were made of yews, and so were diviners' rods. They were the symbol of immortality and were planted beside Bronze Age barrows and, later, in churchyards. The twelfth-century *Book of Llandaf* stated that sanctuary was available to those who sought it 'between the yew tree and the church door'. In 1307, Edward I decreed that yew trees should be planted in every churchyard to protect the fabric of the church from high winds. The trees were often planted in churchyards for their foliage, lethal to grazing animals, in order to keep out cattle. The belief that the practice of planting yew trees in churchyards was encouraged to provide bow-staves from the hard, elastic wood is difficult to substantiate: Welsh archers made their bows of elm rather than of yew.

A row of Irish yews march along the roadside wall of the churchyard.

The avenue of yews leading to the church.

The 'Bleeding' Yew.

The Vitalianus Stone.

The new churchyard was opened in 1930. Its wrought iron gate, bearing the date 1810, was presented by a parishioner.

The antiquity of the site is verified by the presence of early Christian monuments in the churchyard, and in the church. The stone pillar beside the church porch commemorates one Vitalianus whose contemporaries, somewhere around 500 AD, held in such esteem that they carved his name in stone, both in ogham and in Latin. The stone stood, at one time, on the north side of the church[5] and then, by 1859, it disappeared and was later found serving as 'a gatepost on the south side of the high road from Cardigan to Nevern at the entrance to Cwmgloyn Farm.'[6] It was restored to the churchyard soon afterwards, and erected in its present position. The ogham inscription is along the left angle of the face of the stone, reading upwards:

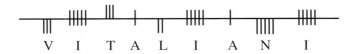

The Latin inscription reads VITALIANI EMERTO, meaning '(the stone) of Vitalianus Emereto(s)'. The second word has been variously interpreted. The Reverend Arthur Wade Wade-Evans, while inspecting the stone, informed the author that he was of the opinion that it was a Roman title granted, rarely, to a British chieftain, or a Briton who had served as a soldier, thus indicating a Romano-British tolerable co-existence. Dr Nash-Williams[7] thought that it was 'presumably a Celticized form of the Latin *Emeritus* which, like *Vitalianus*, was a not uncommon Early Christian name.' He points out that 'the word was also used as an epithet, of one who had "finished his service" here on earth.' Sir John Rhŷs[8] thought that it may have marked the grave of Vitalianus father of Vitalis father of Vortigern.

The continuity of the Christian tradition is proven by the impressive Nevern Cross that stands beside the church. Legend has it that it was being carried by St David to Llanddewibrefi where it was to serve as his memorial and, as he passed by, he called on his friend St Brynach and asked him for some bread and water. St Brynach, however, had taken a fancy to the ornate stone pillar and would only grant David's request if he would leave it behind, which the patron saint reluctantly

The Nevern Cross.

agreed to do. All this regardless of the fact that the saints had been dead five centuries, or so, before the cross was placed there in memory of some very important person.

It is similar to the Carew Cross (SN047037) which can be precisely dated as it commemorates Maredudd son of Edwin who, in 1033, became joint ruler of the kingdom of Deheubarth with his brother Hywel, but was killed two years later. The Nevern Cross is inscribed on the front of the shaft with the Latin inscription h.an.eh which, presumably, was the name of a notable of the eleventh century. On the other side are the letters dns which may be an abbreviated form of the Latin *dominus* (lord).

The monument is of local hard dolerite and is in two parts, the cross-head and shouldered neck being joined by a mortise and tenon joint to the shaft. The front of the cross-head is filled with two-cord twists intercrossing in the centre and is of a type of decoration found on the later Scandinavian crosses in the Isle of Man. The neck has a small panel of interlinked rings. There are five panels on the front of the shaft, from top to bottom: a double-beaded plait; a swastika key pattern, one arm of one swastika being reversed, presumably when the carver was not concentrating; the inscription panel; a loop pattern, and

St Brynach's Church.

a diaper pattern with pellets. The back of the cross-head is decorated in the manner of Northumbrian crosses, and the neck is the same as the front. There are six panels at the back: a band of plain square fret; a short panel of four-cord plait; swastika T-frets; the inscription; a large double Stafford knot, and a diaper key pattern. The sides are filled with panels of plait and knot-work, a swastika T-fret and diaper key pattern.[9]

The cross was scheduled as an ancient monument in 1950.

Churchyard tombstones bear the names of those who have been long dead. Mary Knolles of Wenallt has lain beside the church door 'in hope of joyful resurrection' for three hundred years, and the remains of David Harry of Henllys were buried behind the 'bleeding yew' in 1755, his name carved by Ebenezer Lloyd of Nevern still clear to behold.

High in the north-east corner of the churchyard John Jones, 'Tegid', is remembered by a grey granite cross erected by his admirers.

Along the northern wall the Bowens of Llwyngwair lie, down to the last James Bevan Bowen, sadly killed on his motor-bike. An earlier James Bevan Bowen placed a sundial beside the burials.

The churchyard is older than the church. It was a *llan*, an enclosure, where early Christians were buried, some of them Irish notables, and where Brynach came to establish his house of worship beside the brook Caman, and where the Normans later built their church.

NEVERN CHURCH

The squat tower of Nevern church is all that remains of the building erected during the thirteenth century: the rest is Late Perpendicular, but much restored. The tower is corbelled and battlemented, and there are stepped buttresses on the angles of its west side. A turret on the north-east angle contains a flight of sixty steps that lead to the crenellated roof. There is a four-light window in the west wall and four double-windows with stone louvres light the upper storey.

The church is cruciform in plan and it was described in 1848 as 'an ancient and venerable structure in the Norman style of architecture',[1] but it later suffered from the great activity of church rebuilding promoted during the episcopate of Connop Thirlwall, Bishop of St David's. By the early part of the twentieth century it was found that the church had 'undergone more than one drastic restoration, and a great deal of its character is lost.'[2] The nave, it was stated, had 'been virtually rebuilt' and a gallery at its west end had been removed. The walls of the nave bear memorials to members of the Bowen family of Llwyngwair, with the exception of a brass tablet beside the south transeptal chapel that is inscribed

> TO THE GLORY and famous memory of GEORGE OWEN of Henllys in this parish, Lord of Kemes, who died on the 26th of August 1612 [*rectè* 1613] aged 61 years. He was a Justice of the Peace, a Deputy Lieutenant and Deputy Vice-Admiral of this county and twice served the office of High Sheriff. He was zealous in the performance of all his public duties and in the promotion of the various interests of his native county. He has been styled **Patriarch of English Geologists**; by his *Description of Penbrokshire*, and his other works on the history and antiquities of this county and of the Principality of Wales, he has raised an imperishable monument of his singular learning and industry to his own high renown and to the honour of his beloved county of Pembroke.

The chancel, which is out of alignment with the nave by one degree, was considered by the Cambrian Archaeological Association on its visit to the church in 1922, to be 'particularly interesting on plan

The Norman Tower.

as having recesses for the choir seats upon both sides', both dating from the fifteenth century but 'not coeval with the chancel or with another, and each has been built by a different hand.' The recess on the north side contains the organ, that was presented by the parishioners in memory of those who fell in the 1914-18 war. Some of the side windows were reported to be original, dating from the fourteenth century.[3] George William Griffith of Penybenglog (d. 1654) stated that the coat of arms of Cuhelyn was 'to be seene on the window at Neverne church'.[4] A modern stained-glass window has been placed in the north wall of the chancel in memory of Sir George Bevan Bowen of Llwyngwair who died in 1940, and of his wife, Florence. A tablet on the facing wall commemorates their son, Air Commodore James Bevan Bowen, CBE, Lord Lieutenant of Pembrokeshire 1955-58, who died in 1969. Another tablet in the south wall is a memorial to Edward Warren Jones of Trewern and Llanina who died on 26 May 1829 'in

40

the 71st. year of his age and was buried in his family vault under this church.'

Edward Lhuyd recorded,[5] in 1693, that there was 'an inscription within the church' that seemed to him 'more like Greek than Roman characters' and reproduced, in Camden's *Britannia*, a copy of the inscription that William Gambold, a native of Cardigan but by then of Exeter College, Oxford, whom he assumed 'hath transcribed it with due exactness', had sent to him:

$$V\!/\Diamond I\Diamond \Pi \Pi \Theta I$$

The stone 'was pitch'd on end, not two foot high and is round at top (about which these letters are cut)', he added. In 1896 Lewis Morris maintained[6] that Lhuyd had been given 'a false copy' by Gambold and claimed that the inscription referred to one Iohannes and should be read:

$$_{\diagup O}h\,^{\mathcal{D}}l\!\mathit{l}\,_{\mathit{l}\mathit{l}}\,_{\mathcal{C}\diagup}$$

Morris stated that the stone 'now lies flat in the church', but it has since disappeared.

Dr Nash-Williams has reported that there was in the church 'a roughly shaped rectangular pillar stone inscribed with a Greek cross, with central boss, with equal short limbs dilated at the ends, inscribed within a circle, the two outer incised lines forming which are extended downwards, below the bottom arm, so as to form a long stem or shaft to the cross.' He dated it '7th-9th century (?)' and stated that it was 'apparently now lost'.[7]

The south transeptal chapel is divided from the nave by an arcade of two bays with pointed arches. It has a groined vault which has recently been secured with bronze dowels. A low arched doorway gives access to a spiral staircase leading to a chamber over the vault that is believed to have been a priest's chamber. The Cambrians' report of 1922 stated that 'there was once a drain from the floor, but the whole has been re-roofed, and the interest of the chamber lost by ignorant handling.'[8]

The chapel is known both as the Henllys Chapel and as the Trewern Chapel as the family vaults of these houses lie beneath the floor. A tall

41

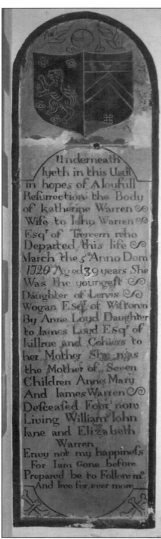

Underneath
lyeth in this Uault
in hopes of A Iouifull
Refurrection the Body
of katherine Warren ℅
Wife to Iohn Warren ℅
Esqr of Trewern who
Departed this life ℅
March the 5th Anno Dom
1720 Aged 39 years She
Was the youngeft ℅
Daughter of Lewis ℅
Wogan Esq of Wifton
By Anne Loyd Daughter
to Iames Loyd Esqr of
killrue and Cohiers to
her Mother She was
the Mother of Seven
Children Anne Mary
And Iames Warren ℅
Defceafed Foir now
Living William Iohn
Iane and Elizabeth
Warren
Envy not my happinefs
For I am Gone before
Prepared be to Follow me
And liue for ever more

Tomb of Katherine Warren.

tombstone commemorates Katherine Warren, wife of John Warren of Trewern and daughter of Lewis Wogan of Wiston, whose 'body lies in this vault in hope of a joyful resurrection.' Above the inscription are the arms of Cuhelyn and a variant on the cognizance attributed to his wife, Gwrangen Feindroed, showing three birds in chief above a chevron between three love-knots which are described in heraldry as 'Bowen knots'. The crossbones are reminders of man's mortality, but the verse provides an assurance of eternal life:

> Envy not my happiness
> For I have gone before;
> Prepared be to follow me
> And live for evermore.

When the Cambrians visited the church in 1904[9] the Archdeacon of Montgomery, the Venerable David Richard Thomas, 'called the attention of the Editor [of *Archaeologia Cambrensis*, Romilly Allen] to a slab with interlaced ornament on it, serving as a lintel-stone of the staircase leading to the priest's chamber above the transeptal chapel on the south side of the nave; and on examining it he was delighted to discover on the adjoining lintel a hitherto unknown Ogham inscription.' When it visited the church again, in 1922, the Association noted with pleasure that the inscribed stone 'had, by the liberality of the late Dr Henry Owen [of Poyston, Haverfordwest], been fixed on the sill of one of the two windows in the Henllys Chapel',[10] and that

Maglocunus Stone.

'the second stone found on that memorable occasion' had also been fixed to the sill of the other window in the chapel. This stone is decorated with an interlaced Latin cross carved in low relief and occupying the length of the stone. The limbs, of plain two-cord twists, are interlaced at the crossing in a characteristic Irish form. The monument is of the early part of the tenth century.[11]

The inscribed stone bears the Latin name MAGLOCUNI FILI CLUTORI indicating that this was the monument of Maglocunus son of Clutorius. The ogham characters, having been incised along the left angle of the face of the pillar, have to be read from right to left: they give the name in the Goidelic form, MAGLICUNAS MAQI CLUTAR[I]. As the Goidelic *maqi* has been used, it is clear that the person commemorated was of Irish origin living in the locality during the fifth, or early part of the sixth, century, at a time when west Wales was ruled by an Irish dynasty.

(I) R A T U L C I Q A M S A N U C I LG A M

The Glastir Chapel, in the north transept, has two piscinae, one of which was attached to a former transept altar and the other to a northern rood altar.[12] A tablet on the north wall of the chapel is to the

43

memory of William Morgan, known by his bardic name 'Penfro', who was born in the parish (see p. 81-2).

A stone[13] found in the south wall of the church in 1860 and reported by Sir John Rhŷs in 1874 to bear the inscription

T	H
V	I
M	I
I	M

was later found to be missing. When it was rediscovered, by George Eyre Evans, it had been mutilated and used in the refitting of the exterior of the second chancel window on the north side of the church for which purpose the upper right-hand portion of the stone, bearing the letters H I I, had been removed. No acceptable interpretation of the inscription has been offered.

A Consecration Cross was found while stripping ivy off the east wall of the Glastir Chapel. Above the central buttress on the outside of the Henllys Chapel is a small Latin cross. A damaged corbel juts from the wall of the Priest's Chamber, above the Vitalianus Stone.

In 1663 it was reported[14] that there were three great bells, with one little bell, in the south transeptal chapel, and one in the church. The tower holds a ring of six bells cast by Thomas Rudhall of Gloucester in 1763. The treble was the gift of the Rev Dr James Philipps who was vicar from 1730 to 1783; the second was given by Thomas Lloyd of

Interlaced Cross.

44

Mounting steps outside the church gate.

Cwmgloyn; the third is inscribed 'Success to our Benefactors'; the fourth was recast to celebrate the 'Victoria Jubilee 1887'; the fifth was presented by the churchwardens, 'Thomas Lloyd, Esqr., Stephen Lewis, gent., Alban Jenkins, Owen Yong'; the tenor, weighing eight hundredweights, is inscribed: 'I to the church the living call & to the grav [*sic*] do summon all: 1763'.

The church plate[15] comprises a large chalice bearing the initials RT attended by two stars and seven pellets probably indicating the maker R Timbrell and dated 1696, which marks are also borne on its paten. The chalice is straight-sided with slight lip and its stem, on a plain moulded base, carries a small knop below the middle. The inscription on the bowl and on the paten states that they were given by 'Anne Colbet of Henthis' which would appear to be an interpretation of Anne Corbet, daughter of Robert Corbet of Ynysymaengwyn in Merioneth, who was the wife of David Owen of Henllys, lord of Cemais. Two credence patens bearing the hallmarks of 1719 with the maker's mark WI beneath two stars and above fleur-de-lys, indicating David Willaume of Pall Mall, are each inscribed 'The Gift of Mrs Martha Griffith daughter of Mr Edward Griffith of Glastir to the Parish of

Nevern in 1733'. In the centre of each is a fully emblazoned coat of arms which appears to be that of the Cope family of Essex. A second chalice, with a bell-shaped cup and with a decorated knop dividing the stem, was presented by Easter Bowen, wife of George Bowen of Llwyngwair, in 1784.

The church was appendant to the barony of Cemais and successive lords of the barony held the advowson. The value of the revenue of the church, with its chapel, probably Cilgwyn, was given in the *Taxatio* of Pope Nicholas in 1291 as £16 annually.[16] This was a considerable sum, twice the value of the church at Newport, and was to be attributed to the fact that Nevern was such a large parish, the largest in the county. When Edward II assigned the advowson to James, Lord Audley, following the death of his uncle, William Martin, in 1326, it was assessed at the equivalent value of 24 marks.

In 1377 Nicholas, Lord Audley and lord of Cemais, was granted a licence by the king to alienate in mortmain the advowson of the church at Nevern to Adam Houghton, Bishop of St David's,[17] who, at the same time, was granted a licence to appropriate the church to the collegiate chantry of St Mary which he, in association with John of Gaunt, had established and endowed with five benefices, of which Nevern was the richest.

Nevern thus became a vicarage,[18] losing the status and income of the rectory. St Mary's College became the rector, and the parish priest the vicar, receiving only about a third of the tithes and being deprived of much of the glebe and the house at Glastir.

The first vicar known to have been presented by the College, John Batty, resigned in 1514 and was succeeded by Thomas ap David ap Jenkin who signed the abjuration of papal authority in 1534.[19]

The *Valor Ecclesiasticus* of 1535 assessed the annual value of the rectory at £27, and that of the vicarage at £8.[20]

John Meyricke was described as 'clerk, vicar of Nevern' when he witnessed the will of James Lloyd of the parish of Nevern, merchant, on 31 March 1551.[21]

At the dissolution of the chantry of St Mary in 1547 the tithes, the glebe and the patronage fell to the Crown, and the tithes were allowed to pass into the hands of laity.[22] The first layman to acquire the lease of the rectory of Nevern was Thomas Howike who paid an annual rent of

£33.14s.8d in 1548. He presented Walter Price, who was instituted vicar in January 1555. William Griffin was presented in 1577.

Richard Edwardes, presented by the Crown in May 1585, had been appointed Chancellor of St David's and Canon Resident in 1571, and was previously sub-chantor of the Cathedral. He lived at Coedwynog where he built himself 'a mansion house' in 1587. He was present at a chapter held at the Cathedral in July 1599, and died the following year.[23]

In October 1596 the lease was granted by the Crown to Thomas Birt, Robert Birt and John Birt, junior, of Llwyndyrus in the parish of Llandygwydd in the county of Cardigan, for the term of their lives at an annual rental of £33.14.8d, and on payment of a fine of £13.6s.8d.[24] Thomas Birt brought several actions against Alban Owen of Henllys, lord of Cemais, charging him with having taken and carried away quantities of wheat, rye and oats in October 1615 which, Birt claimed, were tithes of the rectory of Nevern, but Owen successfully countered that he and his ancestors, time out of mind, had paid the sum of £3.6s.8d yearly in lieu of the tithe of corn and hay.[25]

Richard Edwardes was succeeded by Michael Angell who was presented by the Crown in October 1600. Thomas Prichard, appointed vicar in 1625, was the son of a Pembrokeshire clergyman who had matriculated at Jesus College, Oxford, on 19 June 1610 at the age of nineteen years.[26] He left Nevern in 1628 to become rector of Llangwm and he was appointed Prebendary of Brecon in the following year. His place was taken by Robert Prichard who may, or may not, have been a blood relative.

In 1636 the king, Charles I, granted a lease of the rectory to the Earl of Manchester who, some two years later, conveyed it to Morgan Owen, Bishop of Llandaff.[27] When the bishop died the rectory passed to his son, Owen Owen, and he conveyed it to Owen Price of Llangadog in the county of Carmarthen. Price and Alban Owen were together involved in a suit initiated by William Gibbs of Lincoln's Inn before the Barons of the Exchequer in 1650, according to which Price had assigned the rectory of Nevern to John Reading of the Inner Temple in July 1645 to the use of Gibbs and his assigns for a term of ninety-nine years. The conveyance to Reading was made in consideration that Gibbs absolutely waived the annuity of £120 agreed by Price to be settled on his son,

Marmaduke Gibbs. Gibbs, at great expense, had caused public notice to be given to the parishioners, but Price had promised reward to the vicar, Robert Prichard, if he would announce in church that the title to the rectory was his. Gibbs claimed that the tithes were worth £260 annually. The result of the action is not known.

In October 1662, Oliver Thomas was appointed vicar,[28] but he died shortly afterwards and was succeeded in the following year by John Tucker, MA, the administration of whose goods was granted on 17 March 1692 to his widow. Tucker made an inventory of all things belonging to the church on 11 April 1667. He seems to have been an energetic vicar, and the magnanimity of the parishioners during his ministry is revealed in the range of collections they made for extra-parochial charities which included the repair of the Church of St Alban's (19s.6d), relief of the poor after the Great Fire of London (£1.19s.6d), the relief of poor Christians taken by the Turks (£2.1s.6d), towards Christian slaves in Turkey (£1.11s.10d), and towards Irish Protestants (16s.).

David Jones, presented by the Crown in 1692, was witness to the will of Gwynne Vaughan of Jordanston in Dewisland dated 5 January 1698.

The churchwardens' presentment on 10 June 1708[29] reported that the walls of the church, the roof, the windows and the floor were 'in indifferent good repair', the floor 'being unpav'd as most of our neighbouring country churches are'. A handsome chalice, with a cover of silver, and 'one large flagon' were kept to 'their proper uses'. There was no cloth 'for covering the dead and no box for the poor'. The parishioners were 'promiscuously Welsh and English' and accordingly they had books in both languages. One person lay under the 'heavy judgement of excommunication'. There were 'some very few that frequently repair to private conventicles' and 'none who refuse canonical baptism to their children, unless it be two or three dissenters of late who have found out a new method'. One John Boyd and his wife did not cohabit, and one John Rowland had gone away from his wife. A young man in the parish taught 'some few small children' and instructed them in the church catechism and accompanied them to church 'where they behave themselves quietly and reverently during the time of Divine service and sermon'.

The following[30] were the incumbents thereafter:

1720, July 29	Sutton Morgan, MA, presented by the Crown.
1730, December 23	James Philipps, MA, presented by the Crown.
1783, December 2	David Griffiths, presented by the Crown.
1834, December 4	David Herbert Thackery Griffies Williams, BA, presented by the Crown
1840, October 28	William Davies, presented by the Crown.
1842, April 12	John Jones, MA (Tegid), presented by the Lord Chancellor.
1852, August 7	John Jones, presented by the Lord Chancellor.
1879, June 5	Isaac Hughes Jones, MA, presented by the Lord Chancellor.
1893, September 4	John Owen Evans, presented by the Lord Chancellor.
1911, June 26	Lewis Roderick, presented by the Lord Chancellor.

Following the disestablishment of the Church in Wales on 31 March 1920, royal presentments ceased.

1926, June 1	David Davies, presented by the Diocesan Board of Patronage.
1941, October 23	David John Roberts, presented by the Diocesan Board of Patronage.
1956, June 14	Evan Trefor Jones, presented by the Lord Bishop of St David's
1988, April 16	Bertie Lewis, MA, presented by the Diocesan Board of Patronage, appointed Dean of St David's, 4 March 1990.
1990, August 30	Alan Salmon, presented by the Provincial Board of patronage.
1994, March 13	Bertie Lewis, MA, presented by the Lord Bishop of St David's, following his retirement as Dean of St David's.
1997, June 4	John Pryce Lewis, BA, presented by the Lord Bishop of St David's.

George Owen accounted,[31] in 1600, for eight pilgrimage chapels in the parish of Nevern, as compared with two each in the parishes of Newport and St Dogmael's. Pilgrimage chapels were used during solemn processions on holy days before the break with Rome in the sixteenth century but Owen states that most of the ones in the parishes of Cemais were already ruinous. The Nevern chapels were:

Capel St Thomas, in the Morfa quarter.
Capel St Ffraid (St Bride) in the Crugiau quarter.
Capel Gwenfron, in the Crugiau quarter.
Capel Gwenddydd, in the Crugiau quarter.
Capel Reall, otherwise St Milburgh's Chapel on Banc y Capel (SN071392).
Capel Padrig.
Capel St George, otherwise Capel Cynon on Roft-y-capel (SN055344).
Capel Cilgwyn, dedicated to St Mary, is considered to have been the chapel assessed with Nevern in the *Taxatio* of 1291. The present church was built in 1884.

Cilgwyn Church.

NONCONFORMISM

Early Nonconformists had to meet in private houses or farm buildings, or even out of doors, to avoid persecution. Following the Toleration Act of 1689 accommodation for domestic meetings became inadequate and it was necessary to convert barns or byres, to provide meeting houses or chapels. The architecture of the chapel was based on that of the barn, with doors set in the long side walls, and in the centre of the opposite wall was the pulpit, though some times it was placed between the doors, as at Brynberian and the old chapel at Felindre Farchog. A window behind the pulpit[1] provided a light for the preacher and, it has been suggested, the congregation would see him backlit with a 'halo' of light. Few people could read and they came to chapel to hear *Y Gair*, the Word of God, spoken by one of His elect.

Congregations sought the aid of sympathetic landlords[2] to obtain land upon which they could build their chapel. Where neither gift nor purchase was possible, they negotiated a lease for 999 years, by which

The old chapel at Felindre Farchog.

51

time, they considered, the Millenium would have arrived and chapels would no longer be needed. The building stone was usually obtained, and conveyed, without charge, and so was the timber. The members contributed what they could, often by selling a cow or a calf and donating the proceeds, and it frequently took a considerable time for the required sum to be raised. Between 1689 and 1715,[3] not more than thirty-eight chapels had been built in Wales, four of which were in Pembrokeshire. The difficulty in providing places of worship in rural areas is indicated by the Reverend John Jones (Tegid), vicar of Nevern, in responding to the Religious Census of 1851 when he observed that the distant inhabitants of his parish 'would be leading the lives of heathens had not the Dissenters built chapels in different parts—of which there six.'

Independents

The first chapel established by the Independents in north Pembrokeshire was at Brynberian,[4] in 1690, as a branch of the movement at Llechryd. It was described as 'Presbyterian or Independent' and the chapel had *henuriaid* (elders) who were responsible for doctrine and *diaconiaid* (deacons) who looked after temporal matters, as late as the 1840s. It was in the charge of Thomas Beynon and, after his death in 1728, of David Sais, both of whom were associated with Llechryd, and when David Sais died in 1741, the congregation decided to have its own minister[5] and appointed David Lloyd, of Fachongle, who had officiated as a lay preacher for the previous nine years. He was succeeded at his death in 1764 by his brother Thomas Lloyd until 1770 when Stephen Lloyd was ordained and appointed minister. Stephen Lloyd was described as a wondrously industrious and successful minister who founded branches at Felindre Farchog, Maenclochog and Bethesda, near Narberth, and at Keyston, and the chapel had to be extended to accommodate the increasing numbers in the congregation. In about 1798, however, to the disbelief and mortification of all who knew him, he succumbed to the charms of 'a lady of the neighbourhood'. He was instantly dismissed and despite a display of profound contrition, when he sought compassion and restoration to holy communion, twelve members of the congregation stood in protest. He died in 1801 without ever again receiving the benefit of the sacrament.

Brynberian Chapel.

Stephen Lloyd had been provided with an assistant in Henry George, a native of Nevern, who was ordained in 1790 and officiated until his death in 1840. During his ministry the chapel was rebuilt, in 1808, and it was rebuilt again in 1843. He was the last minister to be appointed from among the membership, as had hitherto been the custom, and he was succeeded by Evan Lewis, a student from the Independent College, Brecon.

The congregation fostered by Stephen Lloyd at Felindre Farchog[6] had built a small chapel, possibly as early as 1786. Like the one at Brynberian, it had two doors on the side wall, and there were three windows between them, the middle one raised so as to benefit the preacher in the pulpit which was situated between the two doors. It was renovated and re-roofed in 1835, and in 1851 it was decided to build a more spacious chapel, Cana, across the road, the foundation stone of which was laid on 17 June 1856 on land given by Sir Thomas Davies Lloyd, lord of Cemais.[7] Stone for the facade was brought from Garn Goediog. The building cost £364.4s.8d and the chapel was opened on 26 July 1857, with special services held on 11 and 12 August in the presence of eighteen ministers, including the Reverend

Cana Chapel, Felindre Farchog.

Caleb Morris, minister of Fetter Lane Congregational Church, London. The old chapel was adapted and was used as a day school until the Board School was opened at Nevern in 1871.

A Sunday School and a monthly service were held at Blaenmeini Farm,[8] where James Davies (Siams Dafi) of Pentregalar 'lodged and preached, Psalm 144, verse 15', during the Association meeting held at Newport on 2 June 1830, 'a rainy night'.[9] In 1844 the venue was removed to Bwlchyfedwen, where a Sunday School was conducted by David Evans of Felinfach, Nevern, and his sons, Stephen, later mayor of Newport, and Benson, who became a Congregational minister in London. Services were also held at Trericert Farm.

In 1859 a Sunday schoolroom was built at Pontgynon in the adjoining parish of Meline for the benefit of the Brynberian members living in that area, and occasional services and prayer meetings were held there. Family devotion was held in most houses in the vicinity, including the Cwmgloyn Arms at Crosswell where, in the absence of any males, the widowed landlady, Mary Rees, led the prayers. John Owen, the author of the ballad *Y Mochyn Du*, who was a servant there before he became a minister, observed that he was glad when there was no man present so that he could enjoy his mistress's intonations.

Methodists

It could be said that Nevern was the stronghold of Methodism in north Pembrokeshire as it found its main patronage at Llwyngwair. George Bowen (1722-1810)[10] was well disposed towards Methodism and had contributed handsomely towards the cost of building the Wesley Room, later the Wesleyan Chapel, at Haverfordwest, at the opening of which, on 18 August 1772, John Wesley preached a sermon. Bowen had previously made it known to George Williams of Pembroke that he would like to meet Wesley, and Williams had informed Wesley to that effect. Wesley preached at Haverfordwest the following evening and the next day, 20 August, he 'rode over to Llwyngwair' where he found 'an agreeable place and an agreeable family' and rejoiced to meet the Reverend David Pugh, rector of Newport, who was a Methodist sympathiser.

Wesley came next to Llwyngwair on Monday, 14 July 1777, having travelled from Carmarthen. He preached at Newport that day and while riding on Newport Sands he was amazed to find 'the roots of trees, leaves, nuts and various kinds of vegetables' beneath the sand and speculated that Cardigan Bay was once dry land. Mr Bowen carried him in his chaise to Cardigan, to preach at noon the next day, and the following morning he preached at Newport before setting off for Trecŵn to have lunch with Admiral Vaughan before proceeding to Haverfordwest. He returned to Llwyngwair on 30 September, hoping that he would be able to borrow Mr Bowen's sloop to sail to Dublin, but he had to go to Fishguard where the 'the captain of a sloop' agreed to take him. Half way across the channel, they were becalmed and Wesley decided to pray. A fair wind sprang up in no time, but it developed into a storm in which, in the pitch dark, he and the captain and a boy had 'much ado to work the vessel'.

On 17 August 1779 he arrived at Llwyngwair to find that Mr Bowen had not returned from a journey to Glasgow but he 'spent a very comfortable evening with Mrs Bowen and the rest of the family.' On Friday, 4 May 1781 he preached at Newport at eleven and again at four o'clock and on the next day he returned to Haverfordwest. He does not say that he spent the night at Llwyngwair but one can assume that he did so. He was there on 19 August 1784 and on 18 August 1788, when he was pleased that a servant of Mr Bowen's had come to guide him from Carmarthen. He stayed on the night of 10 August 1790, on the occasion of his last visit to Pembrokeshire. He was then eighty-seven years of age, and he died the following year.

William Williams, Pantycelyn,[11] whose hymns contributed largely to the revival that began at Llangeitho in 1762, stated in his journal that he and the Countess of Huntingdon and Daniel Rowland travelled from Haverfordwest to Llwyngwair on 2 September 1771, where they enjoyed the company of the Reverend David Pugh, rector of Newport,[12] a living which had been offered to Daniel Rowland and had been declined by him, when Pugh was appointed. In a letter of about 1786 Williams referred to a *Sasiwn*,[13] a meeting of Welsh Methodists, that had been held at Llwyngwair when 'hundreds of people, godly and ungodly, dined and were entertained' by Mr Bowen; 'sixty beds were occupied by strangers at Llwyngwair alone, and about six score sat down to meals there.' When he came again, in 1790, he complained that he was 'ill of the gravel' and was 'obliged to rise 18 or 20 times out of bed each night.'

Williams was a promoter of the Welsh Charity Schools and in his will he bequeathed £100 to George Bowen, among others, to set up such schools and to pay two schoolmasters 'at the rate of £2 for three lunar months'.

He is said to have composed the hymn 'O'er the gloomy hills of darkness'[14] at Llwyngwair while contemplating Carn Ingli in one of its sullen moods. In its translated form, *Dros y bryniau tywyll niwlog*, it became one of the most popular of Welsh hymns.

David Griffiths, who came to Llwyngwair as a tutor, married George Bowen's eldest daughter, and became vicar of Nevern. He was strongly sympathetic to the Methodist cause until it broke away from the Established Church. A Church Chapel built at Nevern in 1799 became the Methodist Chapel in 1811 and remained so until 1876 when it was converted and used as the Board School.

The chapel at Gethsemane[15] was established in 1844 by the Methodists living in the Morfa ward, who were remote from Nevern and cut off from Newport until the bridge was built over the river Nevern. A plot of land measuring 35 yards by 20 yards, upon which to build a chapel, was leased by James Mathias of Treffynnon in 1843. The lease had to be renewed following his death in 1857 and a lease of 999 years was granted by Sarah Mathias, Treffynnon and John Mathias of Tredrysi, of which estate the land formed a part, on 7 July 1866. Four days later, Tredrysi was sold to the Reverend John Jones, vicar of Nevern, and the chapel was included in the sale, but subject to the lease. The rent was paid to the vicar but following the death of Sarah Mathias in 1873, he would no longer accept the rent. The vicar having died in 1879, Tredrysi was sold by his widow to Stephen Hughes of Llechryd in 1885. The conveyance included the chapel but it was omitted from subsequent conveyances and it is thought that a member of the Mathias family had acquired the reversion and presented it to the chapel.

Although the building was completed in 1844, the official opening services did not take place until 1 January 1845. The first Monthly Meeting was held at Gethsemane in October 1847. By the 1860s the Sunday School attendance averaged 95, and the membership was such that worshippers had to arrive early in order to secure a seat at services.

The first minister was the Reverend George Morgan, who was also minister at Tabernacle, Newport. He was assisted by the Reverend Thomas Lamb of Tredrysi who took care of the chapel and its congregation over many years without any payment, and who raised the money required to renovate the chapel, and who will be remembered as the squat little figure forever travelling in his trap and pony and dressed like a vicar, with a round collar and a low-crowned hat.

Baptists

From about 1804 members of Bethlehem Baptist Chapel, Newport, living in the Cilgwyn area, attended prayer meetings at the house of their pastor, the Reverend David Jones, at Penfeidr Cilgwyn. Jones, a native of Nantgwyn, had left to work at the Cyfarthfa Iron Works in Merthyr Tudful where he later entered, and served in, the Baptist ministry until 1802 when he was appointed pastor of Bethlehem. Two years later he married Jane Francis of Penfeidr, where he took up residence and, in order to save his members having to walk to Newport for the weekly prayer meetings, he held them at his house.

From 1829 the meetings were attended by David George who had been granted the tenancy of Trewern farm. George, who had been born in 1809 at Glanllynan in the parish of Ferwig, had been a member of the Sunday School at Bethania Baptist Chapel, Cardigan, where his father was a deacon, and had been baptized by the minister, John Herring. His attendance attracted a bigger attendance at the meetings which, from 1835 onward, were held also at the neighbouring farmhouses of Esgairwen, Llannerch, Plasyffynnon and Fachongle Isaf, where George preached his first sermon. In 1838 he was ordained minister of Jabez Baptist Chapel, Pontfaen.

As the farmhouse meetings continued to expand, consideration was given to the building of a chapel and, at a special meeting held at Penfeidr, it was decided to approach the Trefacwn estate for a plot of land for that purpose. This was secured at a rental of ten shillings per annum for a period of 999 years, and David George obtained the consent of his landlord, Thomas Lloyd of Coedmor, to cut trees to provide the necessary timber for use in building the chapel, which was completed in 1841. The new chapel was called Caersalem and it was

Caersalem.

joined with Jabez under the pastorate of David George. The chapel had to be enlarged in 1870 and by 1882 it had 240 members.

John Llewelyn Morris, a native of Blaenffos, succeeded David George and during his ministry, restoration work was carried out on Caersalem chapel. He died, after a prolonged illness, in 1919. The trustees, in that year, were able to obtain further land from the Trefacwn estate for the purpose of providing a graveyard.

The chapel was then without a minister until 1921 when it appointed J Hendy Davies, a student at Cardiff Baptist College, who officiated as minister for the next twelve years, when the chapel was again without a pastor until 1935. In that year Owen M Young, pastor of Tabor Baptist Chapel, Dinas Cross, was appointed minister and he remained in the office until he died in December 1941 and was buried at Macpelah at Dinas.

In 1943 H J Roberts, pastor at Llwyndafydd and Capel Gwndwn, in the county of Cardigan, was appointed minister. During his ministry the chapel was restored and re-opened in 1948. When he left in 1965 he was followed by Peter Dewi Richards, a native of Felinfoel and at that time a student at Bangor Baptist College. He left after five years and the chapel was again without a pastor until Huw Tudur Jones, a student, was ordained in 1975 and remained as minister until he went to Canada in 1981.

For the convenience of people living in the vicinity of Crugiau,[16] Mary Devonald invited ministers to hold monthly meetings at Trewenfron, when she and her husband moved there in 1778, and continued to do so until she died in 1807, after which meetings were held at Pencnwc and then at Penpedwast, Pantglas, Cwmeog, Pistyll-y-blaidd and Y Rhos, near Llantood Church. In 1819 William Gwion of Rhyd-y-maen offered to lease a plot of land to Blaenwaun upon which to build a chapel at Pencrugiau, but the offer was not accepted until 1824, when Gwion threatened to withdraw the lease, which was for a term of 999 years at ten shillings per annum. The chapel was then built, at a cost of £165, and named Penuel. It was officially opened in October of that year but it was not to become independent of Blaenwaun until it appointed its own minister, Thomas Evans, in 1850. Evans was followed by Daniel Davies who also had charge of Ebenezer Dyfed and was minister during the revival of 1859, when twenty-seven people were baptized one Sunday morning, which led to a demand for the chapel to be rebuilt and enlarged in 1860. Penuel then stood on its own until 1896 when Glannedd Bowen came from Gelli, Rhondda. He and his family resided at St Dogmael's until a manse was built at Bryncemaes. At his death in 1923 he was succeeded by Gwilym Morris who officiated until his retirement in 1942. During the ministry of Tudor Davies, the next pastor, a new vestry was built and the interior of the chapel was restored. In 1958 T R Jones, a student at Trinity College, Carmarthen, was ordained minister and, in the following year, electric lighting and heating was installed in the chapel.

Penuel was joined with the Sunday schools at Ebenezer Dyfed and Bethabara for the Pwnc festival each Whit-Monday. In 1969 it was united with Ebenezer and Penbryn.

NEVERN SCHOOL

A Welsh school was established at Nevern in 1754 by the cobbler-poet Ioan Siencyn,[1] who had been persuaded to do so by Griffith Jones, the educational reformer and rector of Llanddowror. It became an English school in 1780 but Siencyn continued as master until close upon his death in 1796 at the age of eighty years. Griffith Jones had devised a scheme for establishing circulating schools for which he received the patronage of his brother-in-law, Sir John Philipps of Picton, and the support of Madam Bridget Bevan of Derllys, near Carmarthen,[2] who raised most of the money from her affluent friends in London and in Bath. The schools concentrated entirely on teaching children, and adults, to read in Welsh which, although it offered only a limited education, rendered Wales one of the few countries to have a literate majority. When Griffith Jones died in 1761, he bequeathed the funds of the schools and his own private fortune to Madam Bevan for her to carry on with the circulating schools and she, at her death, left £10,000

Nevern School.

for the continuation of the schools. Her will was contested, however, and the money was placed in chancery by George Bowen of Llwyngwair, one of the trustees, and it remained there until 1804 by which time it had grown to £30,000 which was then devoted to the educational purposes originally intended by Madam Bevan.

The Commissioners of Enquiry into the State of Education in Wales visited the village school at Nevern in 1847, and reported[3] that it was housed in 'a wretched schoolroom near the church'. They had received from the vicar, the Reverend John Jones (Tegid), a request that 'Roger's Charity, the cause of discontentment when sharing beef and barley, be paid towards supporting a school master in the parish.' The charity had yielded £22 the previous year. There were only ten pupils present at the school on 26 January, and it may be that the weather was inclement as only five of the thirty-two pupils at St Dogmael's were present the following day. The parochial summary attached to the report reveals that there were two day schools in the parish and nine Sunday schools, most of them being Dissenting Sunday Schools. A Madam Bevan Circulating School was kept at Cilgwyn church.

Advantage was taken of the Education Act of 1870 to improve the low educational standards throughout Wales by establishing Board Schools. A vestry meeting[4] for this purpose was held at Nevern followed, on 23 August 1871, by an election to appoint members of the Board. The Reverend David George, Caersalem, was elected to represent the Baptists; the Reverend Evan Lewis, Brynberian, the Congregationalists; Mr Griffiths, Blaenmeini, the Methodists, and the vicar, the Reverend John Jones, and Mr Thomas Lloyd, Coedmor, to represent the church. Mr Lloyd was appointed chairman, and the Reverend David George, his tenant at Trewern, vice-chairman. Despite differences in outlook, the members of the Board worked in harmony and a Board School was opened at Nevern in 1876, while the school at the old chapel in Felindre Farchog was closed, although the schools inspector had described it as 'the only efficient school in the district'. A Board School was also opened at Cross Roads, near Brynberian.

The Nevern Board School was opened on the site of the old Methodist chapel in 1876 and, shortly afterwards, there were 89 pupils on the register, but the attendance was generally low and averaged about 50 present. Parents had to pay 2d (1p) a week for the education of each child. When the weather was inclement during the early part of the week, the children would be kept at home for the rest, so as to avoid paying the fee.

Education was through the medium of English. The 'Welsh Not' was in use for the purpose of discouraging children from speaking Welsh. This was a rectangular piece of wood in which were carved the letters **W N** and it was hung round the neck of a child heard speaking Welsh until he or she could pass it on to another child caught committing the same sin. The holder at the end of the day was punished. The schoolmaster, from 1878 to 1919, was Alfred Ward, a native of South Shields, who had no knowledge of the Welsh language, and he had the reputation of being a strict disciplinarian. His successor, W J Edwards, came from Glamorgan and was Welsh speaking, and when he retired in 1956 he was succeeded by Lloyd Richards, a native of nearby Newport, who was bilingual and remained in charge until the school was closed in 1961.

The Board School at Cross Roads was opened in 1878 under the auspices of the Nevern Board, and Griffith Miles, a native of Cilrhedyn, was the master from that date until 1910. The school became known as Llwynihirion from about 1884. It had 79 scholars in 1891 but this number had been reduced to 48 by 1913.

NEVERN PARISH COUNCIL

The administration of parish affairs was transferred from the parochial authorities by the Local Government Act of 1894 to Parish Councils and Parish Meetings. On 4 December in that year, at six o'clock in the evening, parish meetings were held simultaneously in each of the four wards of the parish of Nevern. The meeting for the Crugiau ward was held at Cwmgloyn and Daniel Richards of Rhydymaen was appointed chairman. Three nomination papers had been received and, by a show of hands, they were elected Parish Councillors to serve the Crugiau ward on the Nevern Parish Council.

The meeting for the Cilgwyn ward as held at Ty'r Iet when the chairman, David Howells, having received four nominations for three seats, called for election by a show of hands. The candidate receiving the least number of votes then withdrew allowing the other three to be elected councillors.

Nine nomination papers had been received for the Trewern ward and, at the meeting held at Ysguborwen, with Benjamin Rees, Tycanol, in the chair, the names were submitted for election by a show of hands. Although four of the candidates, the required number, showed a substantial lead, a poll was demanded. This took place on 18 December with surprising results: the two candidates who had received most votes at the Parish Meeting were not elected, and the one who had received the least number became one of the four elected Parish Councillors.

The 1894 Act had caused some acrimony as the church was now excluded from involvement in parish government.[1] This became apparent at the Morfa ward meeting held at Tredrysi Fawr. William Williams of Rhosmaen, as overseer, read the notice convening the meeting and proposed that the vicar, the Reverend J O Evans, be chairman, and this was duly seconded and carried. After the vicar had assumed the chair and explained the procedure, Thomas Lamb of Tredrysi, a Methodist preacher, asked him whether they, as ratepayers, were to consider him 'chairman of this meeting to the end, or *pro tem*?' James Marsden of Trellyffant thereupon proposed that the vicar be chairman of the meeting, and he was seconded by Evan Lewis of Blaenmeini. William Morris of Castell-y-garn proposed an amendment that was seconded by William James, Morfa Mawr, that Ebenezer Phillips be chairman and this was carried by fourteen votes to eight. Phillips then took the chair but requested, as his eyesight was poor, that he should be assisted by Thomas Lamb and Evan Lewis. Lamb agreed to the request but Lewis refused. Nomination papers were then received from three candidates who were duly elected. One of the candidates had been nominated by Lamb, and another by Lewis.

NEVERN NOTABLES

For a remote, rural parish, Nevern is not short of people of note, indigenous or immigrant. Vitalianus and Maglocunus were sufficiently important, a millenium and a half ago, to have their names writ in stone, and Brynach the missionary had the church dedicated to him. Cuhelyn is praised in a poem in *The Black Book of Carmarthen*, and his descendants have survived in the leading family of Bowen of Llwyngwair until recent time. Among the remembered sons of the parish are priests and bishops, a hymn-writer and a great Elizabethan historian. Others, who came to Nevern, for the most part as vicars, like David Griffiths and John Jones (Tegid), made contributions that gave them national recognition.

The **Bowens** lived at Llwyngwair for over four hundred years. Sir James ab Owen of Pentre Ifan, a descendant of Gwynfardd Dyfed, who was knighted for his support of Henry Tudor on his way to Bosworth, acquired it from the Cole family (see p. 99) who were said to have arrived with the Normans, for his eldest son by his second wife, Mary Herle, Mathias Bowen.[1] Mathias was married to Mary, daughter of John Philipps of Picton Castle, who, after Mathias's death in 1557, married Hugh Lewis of Nevern, recorder of Cemais.

Mathias was succeeded at Llwyngwair by his son, James Bowen (*c*1543-1629). James, along with his brothers, Thomas and Henry, together with Griffith and John Philipps of Pentypark, was charged with having 'very shamefully and horribly murdered' John Jones of Trecŵn at Newport Fair on 16 June 1578. Griffith Philipps, who had struck the mortal blow with his sword, was hanged and the others were ordered to find sureties for good behaviour. James Bowen failed to do so and disappeared, giving as a reason that he had been pressed to serve on a ship commanded by Sir John Perrot. In 1602, his sons, John and Hugh, were found guilty of killing their cousin, Thomas Young of Tredrysi, in a brawl at Eglwyswrw Fair and they were both hanged at Haverfordwest and buried there. James Bowen, nevertheless, became mayor of Newport in 1604, and again in 1612, and in 1634, when he was seventy-nine years of age, he was appointed sheriff of the county of Pembroke.

Llwyngwair.

George Bowen (d.1660), eldest son of James Bowen, succeeded his father at Llwyngwair at his death in 1629, with his wife Dorothy, daughter of John Scourfield of New Moat. He was sheriff in 1632 and was mayor of Newport from 1640 to 1652. His son, James Bowen (c1591-1677), who followed him, was mayor in 1660 and sheriff in 1671.

George Bowen (1651-1708),[2] the son and heir of James Bowen, married Mary, daughter of Lewis Barlow of Cresswell and, in 1685, he granted a lease of Llwyngwair to his brother-in-law, Richard Barlow of Jeffreyston, but afterwards pleaded that he was delirious at the time and was able to retain his property. He married as his second wife, Dorothy, daughter of Essex Meyrick of Bush, by whom he had a son, James Bowen, who married Alice, daughter of Richard Rowe of Linney, Castlemartin.

George Bowen (1722-1810), eldest son of James and Alice Bowen, added considerably to the estate by his marriage to Easter, daughter and coheiress of William Thomas of Pentowyn, Meidrim, and coheiress also of the Castell Gorfod estate. Furthermore, he purchased a number of properties,[3] mostly in Newport, from Sir John Pakington who had inherited the Perrot estate by marriage. He was mayor of

Cardigan on three occasions, and sheriff of the county of Pembroke in 1803, and he was a Justice of the Peace and a Deputy Lieutenant. Although he was a devout churchman, he was highly sympathetic to the Methodist cause and a number of the early Methodist leaders found an open hearth at Llwyngwair.

James Bowen (1758-1816),[4] son and heir of George Bowen, was five times mayor of Cardigan, and a Justice of the Peace and a Deputy Lieutenant of the county of Pembroke. He married Martha, daughter of Evan Jenkins of Glog, Llanfyrnach, by whom he had two sons.

George Bowen (1800-56), the elder son, was a Deputy Lieutenant and was appointed sheriff the following year. By his wife, Sarah, daughter of John Thomas of Longhouse, Mathry, he had eleven children, the eldest of whom, James Bevan Bowen, born in 1828, graduated at Worcester College, Oxford, and was admitted at the Inner Temple in 1856. He was sheriff in 1862 and mayor of Newport in 1870-72, a Justice of the Peace and Deputy Lieutenant, and was Conservative Member of Parliament for Pembrokeshire during the years 1866-68 and 1876-80. He was chairman of the Pembrokeshire Quarter Sessions and, at the first meeting of the Pembrokeshire County Council, on 16 January 1889, he was appointed Alderman. He died in 1905 and the Nevern Memorial Hall was erected in his memory.

George Bevan Bowen (1858-1940) succeeded his father on his death in 1905, after having received his education at Cheltenham and at Magdalen College, Oxford. He was a Justice of the Peace and Deputy Lieutenant, mayor of Newport in 1913 and sheriff the following year. He was knighted for his public services in 1928. He was married in 1882 to Florence Emma, daughter of Deputy-Surgeon-General Frederick Corbyn, HMIS, by whom he had two sons, one of whom died in infancy, and five daughters.

James Bevan Bowen, the only surviving son of Sir George and Lady Bowen, was educated at Winchester and Trinity College, Cambridge. He was commissioned in the Pembroke Yeomanry and, in 1916, transferred to the Royal Air Force from which he retired in 1937 with the rank of Air Commodore. He was re-employed as Group Captain from 1939 to 1941. He was a Justice of the Peace (1907) and Deputy Lieutenant (1932), and Vice Lieutenant in 1952, and was Lord Lieutenant from 1954 to 1958. He was appointed OBE in 1919 and advanced to CBE in 1958. He married, firstly, Noel, daughter of Leonard Marshall of Nepicar House, Wrotham, Kent, by whom he had three sons, one of whom died young, and three daughters. She died in 1951 and in 1958 he married Muriel Ethelwyn Thomson of Monkton Old Hall, Pembroke, where he died in 1969.

George Bevan Bowen, his elder surviving son, born in 1915, converted Llwyngwair into a guest-house and, later, sold the house which continues to be used as a country house hotel.

David Griffiths, born in 1756 in the parish of Lampeter Velfrey, at Felin Wlân, where his father was the miller, was educated at Pembroke and, when he was eighteen years of age he was appointed tutor to the children of George Bowen of Llwyngwair. Bowen was a supporter of the early Methodists among whom, Howell Harries, Daniel Rowland, John Jones, Llangan and William Williams, Pantycelyn, were frequent visitors to Llwyngwair, and John Wesley came there on no less than seven occasions.

Griffiths entered holy orders and was ordained a deacon in 1779, and a priest the following year, when he was licensed to the curacy of Nevern. He was presented to the living by the Crown in December 1783 and remained there as vicar until his death in 1814, although he is said to have been offered the living of Enfield by Lady Erskine who wrote asking him why he should confine his abilities 'to a parish in Wales when one half of London is thirsting to hear you.'[5]

David Griffiths was one of 'the Methodist clerics' who promoted the Methodist cause as long as it remained within the Anglican church. He, and David Jones, Llangan, travelled through Wales on preaching expeditions, and Griffiths would go to Llangeitho to help Daniel Rowland with the communion when vast crowds gathered there. In 1798 they held a service on Goodwick Sands in thanksgiving for the French surrender there the previous year.

He arranged for chapels to be built in close proximity to the churches at Nevern, Newport, Eglwyswrw and St Dogmael's where weekday meetings were held and in which lay exhorters could preach sermons, until the severance came in 1811. The chapel at Nevern was later expanded for use as the village school.

Griffiths paid occasional visits to London[6] to minister at the

Countess of Huntingdon's chapel at Spa Fields and he was in London when Wesley died, but did not say whether he attended his funeral.

He was a fluent preacher who attracted great crowds wherever he preached. The artist Hugh Hughes recalled that when he preached at St David's Church, Prendergast, Haverfordwest, the churchyard was full of people who could not get into the church to hear him. He had a melodious voice that would easily slide into a *hwyl* that would enchant his audience and was described as as 'an extraordinary preacher, probably the greatest except for Mr [Daniel] Rowland and Mr [David] Jones of Llangan.'[7] Under his ministry Nevern became a centre of the revival, a 'Jerusalem to the inhabitants of Kemes', to which resorted 'Methodist churchmen' from Fishguard to St Dogmael's. He was a handsome man and 'every inch a gentleman' and, in accordance with the custom of the time, he powdered his hair and, later in life, when he lost much hair following a fall from a horse, he wore a wig. He always travelled on horseback and had one of his servants following mounted behind him.

In 1781 he married one of his pupils, Anne, eldest daughter of George Bowen and his wife, Easter. In the pre-nuptial settlement,[8] dated 27 November 1781, the farms of Coedwynog Fawr and Coedwynog Fach were settled and the bridegroom assigned £610 and other monies to which he was entitled, to the bride, whose father secured £1,500 for her. They continued living at Llwyngwair until George Bowen died in 1810, when Griffiths acquired Berllan in the parish of Eglwyswrw, but retained the vicarage at Nevern for his use.

They had seven children: a son, George David, who was educated at Oxford and was made a Justice of the Peace and a Deputy Lieutenant, and died in 1871, and five daughters. Two of the children, who died in infancy, are commemorated in an uncharacteristic verse inscribed on the family tomb:

> They tasted of life's bitter cup,
> Refused to drink the potion up,
> But turned their little heads aside
> Disgusted with the taste and died.

Griffiths took an interest in agriculture at Berllan and became one of the leading farmers of the district. He was for many years a Justice of the Peace and was a strict administrator of the law. He was said to have been conscious of his position and of his wealth, which he inherited when George Bowen died, and was accused of being 'masterful' by nature.

His wife died in 1828, aged 67 years, and six years later, while suffering from depression and when he was beginning to fail, he moved from Berllan to Berry Hill, which George Bowen had purchased from Anne, the widow of Thomas Lloyd of Bronwydd in 1779, and where his sisters-in-law, Elizabeth Alicia and Jane Bowen, were living.[9] In a letter dated 10 March 1834 he described the items of furniture that were to be removed from Berllan to Berry Hill, including a bookcase, a chest of drawers, and an oak box in which he kept all his deeds. He gave instructions to his gardener to send grafts of apple trees—six Lawrence, six Margill, six American, six White Custard, and six Nonpareil, as there were 'few good kinds of apples' at Berry Hill.[10]

On 29 March he wrote to his sister to say that he had been unable to go to Nevern Church during the previous four months and was deprived of the only pleasure he had in this world, which was 'to preach Christ crucified to poor lost man'. He felt 'laid aside as worthless' and would shortly be released 'from this body of sin through the love of God'. Being unable to stand his depression any longer, he took his life by hanging at Berry Hill on 18 September 1834 and was buried at Nevern churchyard in the presence of some three thousand people, who had come to pay their last respects.

When Air Commodore James Bevan Bowen came to live at Berry Hill, in about 1950, he complained to the author that he had been troubled by the ghost of David Griffiths, and had to obtain the services of a priest to exhort it, with bell, book and candle, following which he was troubled no more.

Joshua Hughes,[11] born the son of Caleb and Margaret Hughes of New Mill on 7 October 1807, was educated at Ystrad Meurig and at St David's College, Lampeter. He was ordained deacon in 1830 and appointed curate at Aberystwyth in the following year, and then at Carmarthen before he was appointed vicar of Abergwili in 1838. In 1845 he became vicar of Llandovery. He graduated BD at Lampeter and, in 1870, he was made a DD at Lambeth. In that same year he was nominated by the Prime Minister, W E Gladstone, to the see of St Asaph where he was the first Welsh-speaking bishop to occupy the see for close on 150 years. A number of Church schools were built during his episcopate and he instituted a diocesan board of education. He developed a close relationship with the Nonconformists and insisted upon an adequate provision of Welsh services, both matters that did not endear him to the anglicised and gentry elements in his diocese.

He was married to Margaret, daughter of Sir Thomas McKenny, Bart., by whom he had two sons and five daughters. One son, Thomas McKenny Hughes, FRS, was Woodwardian Professor of Geology at Cambridge and Vice-President of the Geological Society, and the other, Dr Joshua Pritchard Hughes, was Bishop of Llandaff from 1905 to 1931.

He had two brothers, both of whom were clergymen: John Hughes, vicar of Tregaron, and Jacob Hughes, vicar of Llanrhian.

Dr Hughes died on 21 January 1889 and was buried at St Asaph.

John Jenkin, or **Ioan Siencyn**[12] as he was commonly known, was born at Cwm Du, Llechryd, the son of Siencyn Thomas, a dissenting preacher and a poet, who practised his trade as a boot-maker. He learned his father's craft, on which account he was also known as Siôn Crydd Bach, and followed it at Cardigan until 1754, when Griffith Jones, Llanddowror, persuaded him to open a Welsh school at Nevern. It became an English school in 1780 but he remained its master until he was approaching eighty years of age.

In a poem which he wrote in 1782, while he was lying in bed for three months suffering from rheumatism, he stated that he kept school at Cwmgloyn for six years, engaged by Thomas Lloyd to teach the poor to read, the books for which purpose were purchased by Lloyd.

Ioan Siencyn was taught the art of poetry by his father, but he was strongly influenced by the *Gramadeg*. He addressed poems, and elegies, to the local gentry and, in particular, Thomas Lloyd of Cwmgloyn. He was the only poet of standing at the Llanidloes Eisteddfod in 1772, and he made arrangements for an eisteddfod to be held at Cardigan the following year. He was also prominent at the eisteddfod held on Whit Monday 1774 'at the house of John Davies under the sign of the Ship and Castle at Newport, Pembrokeshire.'[13]

One of his poems celebrates the formation of a friendly society at 'Tafarn-y-bwlch yng Ngwyddfa'r Cilgwyn', and several are traditional begging poems, one seeking a pair of boots for his gout-swollen feet, and another a periwig to cover his bald pate. He wrote 'a song to Squire Lloyd of Cwmgloyn's new ship', the *Greyhound*,[14] launched at Aberystwyth but trading from Newport under Captain Tucker of Sealyham, and another on the launching of the schooner *Hawk*,[15] of fifty tons, at Newport. This poem was chosen by Saunders Lewis in a broadcast talk on 'The Essence of Welsh Poetry'[16] to illustrate 'the literary tradition of Wales' where he states that 'you cannot pluck a flower of song off a headland in Dyved in the late eighteenth century without stirring a great Northern star [Taliesin] of the sixth century' and adds that 'the whole body of Welsh poetry from the sixth century onward has contributed directly to Ioan Siencyn's verses.'

He died in 1796 and was buried at Llangoedmor.

John Jones (**Tegid** or sometimes **Ioan Tegid**)[17] was born at Llanycil, on the shore of Llyn Tegid, on 10 February 1792, the son of Henry Jones and his wife, Catherine. He was educated at more than one school at Bala before entering the grammar school attached to the Presbyterian Academy at Carmarthen. He was here, and at another school in that town, for brief periods before returning to Bala where he attended 'several schools' before proceeding to Jesus College, Oxford in 1814. He graduated, with 'second' in mathematics, in 1818 and proceeded MA in 1821. He had planned to take up a teaching post at a college in Calcutta but, instead, he took holy orders and became chaplain of Christ Church, Oxford, and precentor there in 1823 and was presented to the perpetual curacy of St Thomas where he established a school for boys and girls.

On 27 August 1841, through the influence of Lady Llanover, he was presented with the living of Nevern by the Earl of Cottenham, Lord Chancellor, and was instituted on 12 April 1842.[18] He was collated prebendary canon of St David's in 1848.

As a young man, at Bala, he mastered the traditional Welsh prosody under his mentor, Robert William of Y Pandy, Tre Rhiwedog, poet and farmer who had been a pupil of Rolant Huw. He does not rank high as a poet, and yet Professor T Gwynn Jones declared that 'he will be remembered as long as the Welsh language survives as the author of *Ymweliad y Bardd a Thref y Bala.*[19] The poem was translated by Lady Charlotte Guest as *The Bard's Journey to Bala.*

A collection of his poetry, together with a biography, was published by his nephew, the Rev Henry Roberts, in 1859 in the volume *Gwaith Barddonawl.*

Tegid came under the spell of William Owen Pughe's new orthography and in 1820 he published a tract, *Traethawd ar Gadwedigaeth yr iaith Gymraeg* in support of Pughe's notions. In 1829 he published *A Defence of the Reformed System of Welsh Orthography.* With Gwallter Mechain, he edited the poems of Lewis Glyn Cothi, and wrote a historical introduction in which he was led astray in his treatment of the poet by his adherence to Pughe's orthography and etymologizing, and this also affected the edition of the New Testament he prepared for the Society Promoting Christian Knowledge and led to the abandonment of the publication of the Old Testament in the same orthography. He was one of the translators of the Report of the Commission on Education in Wales which was published in 1848.[20]

In 1830 he published a new version of the Book of Isaiah which received the plaudits of the Hebraists and went into a second edition.

Tegid was active in the eisteddfodic promotions of 'the literary clerics' and he was present at a Gorsedd ceremony held at Kerry in January 1821 where he and Y Bardd Cloff (Thomas Jones: 1768-1828) were admitted as Bards.[21] When Eben Fardd won the chair at the Liverpool Eisteddfod in 1840, at the Gorsedd ceremony that followed he took the sword in his right hand 'while Tegid tied a blue ribbon round his arm above the elbow' to signify that he had been admitted into the Order of Bards. When the gentry of north Wales did not appear to be ready to support the holding of an eisteddfod at Bangor in 1853, Tegid suggested that the people of Bangor should promote their own eisteddfod without relying on the help of others.

There is no record that he was present when Cymreigyddion y Fenni was formed at Abergavenny in 1833 to promote the Welsh language and culture, or that he was at the first eisteddfod held in November 1834. His presence was noted, however, at the Eisteddfod held in October 1837 and again in 1838 when he and Rhydderch

Gwynedd led le Vicomte Villemarqué, who led a Breton delegation sent by Louis Philippe of France to collect information relating to old Welsh manuscripts, to be admitted into the Gorsedd by the presiding bard, Cawrdaf.

The main patrons of the Abergavenny eisteddfodau were Sir Benjamin Hall and his wife Augusta, the future Lord and Lady Llanover. Augusta Hall introduced Tegid to Lady Charlotte Guest soon after she had married Josiah John Guest and had come to live in Dowlais in 1833.

Lady Charlotte Guest, in her diary,[22] states that she and her husband attended a concert on the evening of 27 October 1837 at which Tegid 'danced a curious pantomime Welsh dance, not very interesting, and representing a tipsy man going home and crossing a brook on which occasion he takes off his hat and coat and shoes, and afterwards resumes them . . . The evening was altogether very pleasant and spirited. Tegid was so pleased with Yr Eos Fach singing that he composed an englyn in her honour on the spot.' Yr Eos Fach (the little nightingale) was 'a little girl from Merthyr' who sang earlier in the programme.

Tegid provided Lady Charlotte with a transcript that he made from *The Red Book of Hergest* in the library of Jesus College, Oxford. She translated the *pedair cainc* (the four branches) of the Mabinogi— Pwyll Pendefig Dyfed, Branwen ferch Llŷr, Manawydan fab Llŷr and Math fab Mathonwy—and an additional seven other prose tales of a later date, which she called *The Mabinogion*.

On 30 November 1837 she recorded that Sir John Bernard Bosanquet of Dingestow Court, a retired judge, had agreed, through Tegid, to lend her his copy of *Llyfr Coch Hergest* which she hoped 'to publish with an English Translation, notes, pictorial illustrations. Price [Carnhuanawc] and Tegid have promised their assistance, and by God's blessing I hope I may accomplish the undertaking.'

On 4 December she heard that the MSS Society wanted to take *The Mabinogion* into their own hands, 'but we have to arrange to prevent this,' she said. Tegid came that day and took away the Bosanquet MS 'to copy from it one story at a time in a fit manner to go to the Press, viz: in Modern Orthography which would be more generally useful, and send them to me to translate.'

When Villemarqué came to Abergavenny, and spent New Year's

day at Dowlais and took such an interest in *The Mabinogion* that he wanted to publish one of the tales, 'Peredur', in France, she hastened to complete her translation of it so as to 'get it out in London before the Frenchman could do so in Paris.'

On 9 April she complained that although she had 'twice written to beg Tegid to get me a facsimile from the Llyfr Coch, he has given me no answer.' He had promised to copy for her 'all the Mabinogion in the Llyfr Coch which are not in the collection I print from. It would be a great advantage,' she continues, 'if he would correct the Press of Peredur, but I hesitate asking him. I am not sure if he may be safely trusted with the secret of my proceeding,' that being its speedy publication to forestall Villemarqué.

Lady Guest translated Tegid's best-known poem, as 'The Bard's Journey to Bala',[23] and it was later published, along with the original poem, by J D Jones of Ruthin, in a popular series of sheet music and sold for 3d.

Tegid's admiration of William Owen Pughe led him to persuade the University of Oxford to grant Pughe the honorary degree of a Doctor of Common Law in recognition of his work in general and particularly for his translation of Milton's *Paradise Lost*, a copy of which he presented to Tegid on the day of the convocation.[24]

An article published in a local newspaper[25] to commemorate the centenary of his death claimed that 'Tegid still lives in the memory of the generations which have followed, as a noble character and a true Welshman,' and it recalls an incident when Tegid was 'walking to Newport through Sandy Lane one dark night' and, placing his hand on the latch of the gate entering the lane, another hand from the opposite direction was placed on his hand. 'Pwy sy 'na?' came a startled cry from the unknown person. Quick came Tegid's reply:

> Ioan Tegid yw fy enw,/ Peidied neb ag ofni hwnnw,
> Nid oes ganddo arf na chleddyf / Dim i'w arbed ond ei goesau.

> (Ioan Tegid is my name: let no one fear it. It has no weapon or sword to protect it, only its legs.)

The article also quotes a verse from Tegid's *Ymladd Cressi* (the Battle of Crecy), and an admonishing verse which he had composed a few weeks before his death.

Tegid's tomb.

Nevern Vicarage, showing vine given to Tegid by Lady Llanover in 1848.

78

While he was lying on his death-bed, according to a report that appeared in *Y Brython* some years after he had died, 'on the morning of the Lord's Day, while a neighbouring clergyman was taking the service for him at Llanhyfer [*sic*] Church, the voice of the reader was suddenly drowned by the beautiful song of a thrush, that filled the whole church . . . It was ascertained on leaving the church that at that very moment the soul of Tegid left his body for the world of spirits.' Again, on the day of his funeral, the same bird was said to have sung from the bough of a tree 'as the coffin was lowered to its resting place as if to pay homage to the Christian gentleman who had endeared himself to members of the feathered world.'

The grey granite tombstone erected over his grave in Nevern churchyard is inscribed:

> Isod y gorffwys gweddillion marwol y Parch John Jones, M.A., (Tegid), offeiriad, bardd, ysgolor a gwladgarwr ffyddlawn. Periglor y plwyf hwn 1842-1852. Prebendar Tyddewi 1848-1852. Ganwyd Chwefror 10 1792. Bu farw Mai 2 1852. Cyfodwyd y golofn hon yn 1908 gan ei edmygwyr.

Outside the vicarage at Nevern grows a vine off which I ate my first grapes. Tegid recorded,[26] on the back page of the Burial Register (1813-69), that the vine had been given to him by Lady Llanover during the Abergavenny Eisteddfod of 1848 and he added the following verse by Bedo Aeddren (fl. 1500):

> Y winwydden a nyddir
> Yn egwan iawn, yn ir;
> Os bydd hen y gangen gu
> Ni oddef mwy ei nyddu.

(The vine may be spun while it is weak and green, but when it becomes a strong branch it will not stand being spun.)

Evan Lloyd,[27] described as a Baptist Unitarian minister, was born at Nevern on 21 March 1764. He became a member of the Baptist Chapel at Cardigan and assistant to its founder, William Williams, JP, who had married Jane, daughter of James Bowen of Llwyngwair. He served in the militia when the French landed at Fishguard in 1797. In

1801 he was ordained at Ffynnonhenri, Cynwyl Elfed, but was soon converted to Arminianism and joined the General Baptist cause of *Tŷ Coch* at Cardigan and he was pastor there and at Zoan Chapel. By 1808 he was minister of the two General Baptist churches at Wick and Nottage in Glamorgan, where he remained until his death on 30 July 1847. He became a declared Unitarian when he was beyond sixty years of age and attended Unitarian, as well as the General Baptist, assemblies. He was succeeded at Wick and Nottage by his son, and then by his grandson, and then by another descendant, so that the pastorate remained in the family, except for a short break, for a hundred and twenty years.

John Lloyd, MA, DD,[28] Suffragan Bishop of Swansea, was born in Nevern in 1847. His father, William Lloyd, was the son of Stephen Lloyd of the Trewern Arms and his wife, Elizabeth Mathias. He graduated at Cambridge and was appointed curate of Rockhampton in 1876, and afterwards of Stovington. He became vicar of Llanfihangel Aberbythych, and then of Penboyr, and was collated Prebend of Treflodan at St David's Cathedral on 23 June 1890. The next day he was installed vicar of St Peter's, Carmarthen, and consecrated Suffragan Bishop of Swansea by the Bishop of St David's, Dr Basil Jones. In that office he assisted Bishop Jones for the next seven years and then served Bishop Owen in the same capacity for another eighteen years. He was appointed Treasurer of the Cathedral on 7 May 1899, and was admitted Canon on the same day. He remained vicar of St Peter's, Carmarthen, until 18 January 1901, when he was appointed vicar of Jeffreston. He resigned on 30 September 1903 and was appointed vicar of Lampeter and, then, in 1908, vicar of Cantref in the county of Brecknock. He had resigned from the treasurership of the Cathedral in January of that year. He died on 10 June 1915 and was buried at Mumbles.

Thomas Lloyd,[29] the only son of Thomas Lloyd of Cwmgloyn by his wife Anne Scourfield, succeeded his father at Cwmgloyn. He was a Justice of the Peace and Sheriff of the county of Pembroke in 1771. He was mayor of Cardigan in 1769 and again in 1778.

He was regarded as a progressive farmer and the owner of three vessels, two of which, the *Hawk* and the *Greyhound*, featured in poems by Ioan Siencyn

He died without issue on 28 January 1788 and was buried at Bayvil. He devised his estate to Morris Williams, son of Evan Williams of Trellyffant who was a son of Morris Williams of Cwm Betws by his wife Frances, daughter of Evan Lloyd, a younger brother of George Lloyd of Cwmgloyn, who was the Sheriff in 1696. Morris Williams, who was Sheriff in 1815, died without issue, and Cwmgloyn passed to his nephew Owen Owen, Sheriff in 1848, who married Mary Anne, daughter of Morgan Rice James of Haverfordwest, solicitor. Owen died at Berllan on 11 February 1849 and Cwmgloyn was inherited by his son, Morris William Lloyd Owen, who was educated at Eton and St John's College, Cambridge. He was a Justice of the Peace and a Deputy Lieutenant, and was Sheriff in 1870. He married Grace Caroline Mary, daughter of Wilberforce Pearson, and died without issue in 1907. He and his wife lived at Kent House, Haverfordwest, where the 'Trellyffant Toad' was last seen.

Stephen Llwyd,[30] born at Llystyn Bach the son of Joseph and Elizabeth Lloyd, in 1794, received some education, probably at Nevern, before entering his father's trade as tailor. He was given instruction in music by Dafydd Siencyn Morgan, precentor of Capel Isaf Congregational Chapel, Llechryd, who travelled the district teaching music. He settled at Fishguard where he was appointed precentor at Hermon Baptist Chapel and gained a reputation as a musician throughout the county. He moved to Pontypridd in 1840 and was precentor at Carmel Baptist Chapel in that town until he died in April 1854, and was buried in the chapel burial ground.

His hymn-tune 'Caerllyngoed' appeared in *Seren Gomer* in 1822 in which journal were also published his 'Abergwaun', 'Taf' and 'Rhondda', whilst his 'Carol Nadolig' appeared in *Cronicl y Cerddor* in 1882.

William John Morgan,[31] cleric and hymn-writer known by his bardic name 'Penfro', was born at Nevern on 14 December 1846, the son of David Morgan who, soon after, removed to Boncath where he was parish clerk and precentor at the church at Llanfihangel Penbedw.

William was educated at the Cardigan Grammar School and at St David's College, Lampeter, where he graduated BA in 1871. He was ordained that year and licensed to Llanrwst where he became acquainted with the poet Trebor Mai and the eccentric Gwilym Cowlyd who established a rival Gorsedd of Bards in which he appointed Penfro Chief Druid. He, on that account, had no connection with the National Eisteddfod but he was prominent in the provincial Powys Eisteddfod. He was curate at St Asaph from 1875 to 1878, when he was made vicar of Pennant, in Montgomeryshire, and then, in 1887, vicar of Llansanffraid Glan Conwy. In 1904 he was appointed rector of Manafon, where Gwallter Mechain had once been incumbent and the poet R S Thomas was to be. He died there on 23 June 1904, his wife and two of his four children having predeceased him. A tombstone, and a tablet in the church, commemorate his name. *Penfro: Cyfrol Goffa*, a volume containing his hymns and some of his poems, together with a short biography, was published in 1924.

George Owen,[32] son of William Owen (p. 83) was born at Henllys in 1552 and probably received his early education from his father. He was admitted at Barnard's Inn on 5 August 1574 but by that time he was married to Elizabeth, daughter of William Philipps of Picton Castle by his wife Janet, daughter of Thomas Perrot of Haroldston and sister of Sir John Perrot. Elizabeth Owen, having given birth to eleven children, died in 1606 and, soon after, Owen married his mistress, Anne, or Ankred (Angharad) Obiled, of Carmarthen, who had already borne him seven natural children and was to bear five more after marriage. Owen was a progressive farmer, advocating the use of fertilisers, particularly marl, or glacial till. He was the first person to trace the basic geological features of Pembrokeshire and to establish that the same series of rocks succeed each other, which led to his description on the commemorative plate in Nevern church, as 'Patriarch of English Geologists', a quotation from *The Edinburgh Review*.[33] His map of Pembrokeshire was used by William Camden in his *Britannia*.

He succeeded his father as lord of Cemais and was much involved in litigation on account of his claims to manorial franchises. His efforts to establish a descent from the Norman invaders of Cemais caused him to be accused of 'creative genealogy'.

He was a Justice of the Peace, and he and Thomas Perrot were the first Deputy Lieutenants appointed for Pembrokeshire. He was sheriff in 1587 and in 1602, and was deputy vice-admiral for the counties of Cardigan and Pembroke. He was influenced by the awakening of interest in antiquities that took place in his time and gathered a coterie of antiquaries around him. He was a generous patron of the bards and of learning generally. He was a prolific writer and a leading Elizabethan historian, remembered particularly for his *Description of Penbrokshire* (1603) first published in 1892, edited by Henry Owen and again, in modern spelling, in 1994 by the present writer

William Owen (*c*1488-1574) was the son of Rhys ab Owen Fychan of Henllys by his wife Jane, daughter of Philip Elliot of Earwere and his wife Janet, daughter of Sir Thomas Perrot of Eastington. Jane had previously been married to Philip ap Gwilym of Stone Hall who had died leaving her with a family of four young children. William was probably born at Stone Hall. He was admitted to the Middle Temple in 1514 and, in 1521 he published a book on the abridgement of the laws of England. By then he owned property in Pembroke and was mayor there in 1527. He practised law in that town and in Bristol and in London, where he married a widow, Margaret Henton. She died without leaving issue, though William had nine children by various concubines. In 1551 he married Elizabeth, daughter of Sir George Herbert of Swansea, whose brother became Earl of Pembroke. By her he had a son, George, the historian, and a daughter, Katherine, who married Owen Johnes of Trecŵn. While he was in London he met John Touchet, Lord Audley and lord of Cemais, who had recovered the sequestered estates of his attainted father. He appointed Owen clerk of the courts of Cemais and borrowed money from him against the security of the barony, which was conveyed to Owen in 1542 when Audley bade his tenantry henceforth to 'obey the said William Owen as their very lord and right owner of the said barony.'

William Owen,[34] born in 1750 the son of Joseph Owen of Frongoch, was ordained deacon in 1773 and priest in 1775, in which year he was appointed curate at Nevern where he remained for the next four years. He succeeded Thomas Charles 'of Bala' in the curacy of Sparkford in 1783 and then of Milbourn Port in Somerset in 1785. In 1816 he was presented by the Bishop of Hereford to the vicarage of Almeley and in 1823 he received the rectory of Ryme Intrinsica, near Sherborne, the patron of which was the Prince of Wales, later George IV. He was an active supporter of the Church Missionary Society. He frequently visited his native county and, when his father died, he inherited Frongoch.

William Rogers,[35] who became a prosperous businessman in London with a 'messuage, shop and premises in High Street, Kensington', and is described as 'of Kensington in the County of Middlesex, Gentleman', in his last will and testament, proved on 19 July 1806, devised all that part of his 'estate situated on the south side of Vidar [Feidir] Saint in the Parish of Nevern in the County of Pembroke called Penrallt' to his mother, Elinor Rogers, for the term of her natural life and thereafter to his sister, Margaret, wife of Lewis Rees, and then to their son, John Rees, and the other part of the estate, lying north of Feidir Saint, to his brother James and his heirs. He left £40 to his servant, Jane Satter; 20 guineas to his cousin Sarah Edwards, housekeeper to the Duke of Marlborough; £10 to David Davies, Kensington, watchmaker, and to William Knight of Kensington, attorney-at-law, and five more of his friends, 'a handsome mourning ring each as a token of my esteem for them.' He desired, should he die within a hundred miles of London, that he be buried 'under the same stone where the remains of my late wife and sister Elinor are buried in the churchyard of the parish of Kensington,' but if he should happen to die beyond the hundred miles, or in Wales, his body should be interred in the grave with his sisters Ann and Elizabeth in the churchyard at Nevern 'in a plain but decent manner'. He is not buried there, and there is no memorial to him.

In his will Rogers also bequeathed 'unto the Minister and Church Wardens of the Parish of Nevern, and their successors for the time being for ever, Eight Hundred pounds Stock in three per cent consols' from the interest and dividends of which should be 'laid out annually in manner following, one Moiety thereof in good Beef and the other Moiety thereof in good Barley and the same to be distributed on every Saint Thomas's Day [21 December] in every year by the Minister and

Church Wardens of the said Parish.' There is no direction as to beneficiaries, and no requirement that its administration should continue 'as long as water flows under Nevern Bridge', as is frequently stated.

The distribution has been regularly conducted since 1806, except for the years of the last war and the subsequent period of food rationing. In 1848 the dividend amounted to £24 and benefits were distributed 'in shares of between two and three gallons of barley and two or three pounds of beef'. An account of 1895 shows that 505 lbs of beef had been purchased at six pence a pound and 50 bushels of barley at 3s.4d a bushel and this, together with a small expenditure on refreshments for the vicar and church wardens, accounted for the income of £25.5s.4d (£25.27). The beneficiaries numbered 124. In 1993, beef to the value of £35.51, and a token amount of barley, was distributed to nine beneficiaries.

NEVERN 1600

As soon as he had completed *The First Booke of the Description of Penbrokshire in generall*, to give it its full title, George Owen began work on 'the second booke', which was to be a detailed history of the county, parish by parish. But he was unable to make any progress beyond the lordship of Cemais. A fragment comprising twenty-one folios covers eleven of its parishes, and others may have been described on folios that are known to be missing. The folios were discovered among Bronwydd papers deposited at the National Library of Wales during the last war by Dr B G Charles who published an annotated version in *The National Library of Wales Journal*, 1948, pp. 269-277.

The folios devoted to the parish of Nevern refer to fifteen of the twenty-two gentry residences within the parish and these are situate in the Crugiau, Morfa and Trewern quarters: the Cilgwyn quarter was not completed. Several of the houses were built, or rebuilt, during Queen Elizabeth's reign and Owen provided approximate dates for them, e.g. Llwyngores *c*1574 and Coedwynog *c*1588.

The folios relating to the parish of Nevern, rendered in modern spelling, are as follows:

Nevern

Nevern is the greatest and largest parish in the shire and takes the name of the river Nevern . . . In Welsh it is called *Y Nyfer* and in old time was dedicated to the British saint called Saint Brynach whose festival day is yet duly observed within this and diverse other parishes with no small solemnity the seventh day of April, on which day that is with us said, the cuckoo first begins to tune her lay. I might well here omit an old report fresh as yet of this odious bird that in the old world the parish priest would not begin Mass in this parish until this bird (called the Citizen's Ambassador) had first appeared and begun her note upon a stone called Saint Brynach's stone being a stone curiously wrought with sundry sorts of knots standing upright in the churchyard of this parish, and one year staying very long and the priest and people expecting her accustomed coming (for I account this bird of the feminine gender) came at last and lighting upon the stone her accustomed preaching place and being scarce able once to sound the note upon the said stone presently fell down dead. This religious tale although it concerns in some sort church matters you may either believe or not without peril of damnation. The Rectory of this parish was some time an advowson appendant to the Lordship of Cemais & given or sold by Sir Nicholas de Audley, sometime lord of the said lordship, to Adam Houghton bishop of Saint David's by a charter dated on the Feast of Saint Margaret in the first year of Richard II [1377] who did impropriate the same to the new College of Saint Mary in Saint David's which appeared by the king's licence obtained for the mortmain with these words *Reseruando semper prefato Nicholao et heredibus suis Ius patronatus ecclesiae predictae*, so that the Right of the patronage of the said church yet remains appendant to the said Lordship of Cemais.[1] It is now the king's inheritance upon the senseless suppression of the said College and now pays His Majesty of rent £33 13s. 4d. The cure is discharged by a vicar erected upon the impropriation which the late prince Queen Elizabeth has of late years presented *De facto non de iure* and has for his part *quartam partem fructuum* & is valued in the books of first fruit £8.

Four Quarters

This parish in respect of the greatness thereof is divided into four though unequal parts, each of them having a Constable & Churchwarden respectively the one not intruding in the other's part, the names of which quarters are these *Crugiau* and *Morfa* in north Nevern, *Trewern* and *Cilgwyn* in south Nevern, in which four quarters I will severally treat of the most notable places & matters in the same, and first I will begin with Crugiau quarter as that which is the first in the way I hold.

Henllys[2]

Henllys, the mansion house of George Owen the author of this idle work, is seated in this quarter of Crugiau upon a bank towards the south with a deep & steep descent to the river of Nevern which runs south thereof through a deep and pleasant valley. This house demesnes

& is in effect an island in dry land for that the same is round about (one little space as that were left for a bridge) compassed with deep valleys and steep hills to ascend to the same. Henllys in Welsh signifies the *Old Court* or *Palace* & is of so ancient descent to the now owner & his ancestors that although for diverse hundred years past the same by ancient evidences appears to be theirs, yet the first original does not by any matter appear how or when the same first came or that ever any other family or person than his ancestors owned the same. It appears that in the time of Henry III one Nesta the daughter and heir of one Llywelyn ap Rhydderch, a younger son of the prince of south Wales, was heir thereof, who bestowed herself this & the rest of her fair inheritance upon Philip ap Richard the son of one Richard de Hoda who married the daughter and heir of Sir Nicholas Martin, lord of Cemais[3] . . . This Philip ap Richard had issue, Philip Fychan, father to Philip father to Ievan ab Owen father to Owen Fychan ab Owen father to Rhys ab Owen father to William Owen father to this George Owen, as appears by fair & ancient evidences & writings continuing the aforesaid descents from the time of the said Nesta hitherunto. The mother of the said George Owen was daughter to Sir George Herbert of Swansea, her mother a Berkeley and hers a Neville. Sir George Herbert's mother was the sole heir of Sir Mathew Cradock and her mother a Mansel. The mother of the said William Owen was daughter to Philip Elliott, her mother a Perrot & hers a Picton, the mother of Philip Elliott a Barrett. He bears *gules* a boar *argent* chained to a holly bush proper armed & unguled *or* & chain the colour of the last. The wife of the said George Owen is Elizabeth daughter and coheir of William Philipps of Picton, esquire. The second [wife] Anne the daughter of John Gwillim a French gentleman of ancient descent in Normandy by Elizabeth the daughter of Sir Alexander Phitton of Gosworth in Shropshire.[4]

Cwmgloyn[5]

Cwmgloyn (the mansion house of Ievan Lloyd son and heir to John Lloyd of Hendre . . . Saint Dogmael's) is so called of the valley where it stands of like name. This in ancient time was the land of Gwallter ap Rhys ap Rhydderch father to Peter commonly called Perkin ap Gwallter father to Gwilym Perkin father to David Gwilym Perkin

88

father to Jane his daughter and heir who married Owen Lloyd grandfather to the said Ievan, and so now is his by ancient descent, & now having occasion to speak of the aforesaid Rhys ap Rhydderch . . . you shall know that the said Rhys father to the forenamed Gwallter was owner of this house Cwmgloyn as also Crugiau Isaf, Penybenglog & Glanduad Uchal in Meline being now four several mansion houses of men of sort & to be spoken of here & in other places. And first to speak of Crugiau Uchaf being next to hand. The said Gwallter had also a son called Llywelyn father to Gruffydd father to Owen father to Lewis ab Owen Griffith who diverse years past pawned the said house & lands of Crugiau to Thomas Young of Tredrysi father to Philip Young father to John Philip Young who now dwells there. The arms of the Youngs you shall find under Glastir.

Also the said Rhys ap Rhydderch had a younger son named Gwilym ap Rhys who had to his part the two houses of Penybenglog and Glanduad aforesaid, which Gwilym had Llywelyn who also had two sons David ap Llywelyn and Rhys ap Llywelyn. David had Penybenglog whose sole daughter and heir, Dyddgu, married Rhys David Powell father to Thomas father to Griffith Thomas father to William Griffith[6] who now enjoys it & is his mansion house.

Glanduad Uchaf[7]

To the other brother Rhys ap Llywelyn he gave Glanduad Uchaf whose only daughter and heir, Morfydd, married Rhydderch Warren & had issue Margaret Rhydderch their only heir wife to Owen ap Mathias ab Owen of Ricardston who gave this Glanduad to their second son Thomas Bowen who did the like to his second son Ievan ab Owen who now dwells there.

Llwyngores[8]

Llwyngores the mansion house of Mathias Bowen gentleman stands for health and pleasure fair upon the top of a bank overlooking a fair and pleasant valley being the more pleasant for that it is his own. This house was built about 30 years past by his elder brother Thomas George Bowen a man who for his good hospitality gentle behaviour among his equals, his good advice to his distressed neighbours & other his good parts, was much lamented at his death, who having issue but one daughter sold the same to this her uncle being third son to his father George Bowen a man in his time of no small rule & estimation who was the natural son of John Bowen son & heir of Sir James Bowen knight & bears the arms of Pentre Ifan with the due difference.

Coedwynog

Coedwynog was the mansion house of Mr Richard Edwardes, Chancellor of Saint David's, deceased & by him built about 16 years past & much beautified being the first man that caused the place to be accounted or spoken of, although there was some pretty buildings there before his time yet nothing to which he left behind him. This man for his discreet behaviour courteous & liberal entertainment in his house, his grave & well advised counsel to men of all sorts & for his natural inclination, his facile method in peace making, is not a little missed in his country; his only noted fault in his lifetime was too much levity in not bearing himself as his place & calling required. This good man had made this his house to be in account as says Cicero: *Non domus dominum sed dominus domum exornat.*

Morfa

Morfa quarter comes next to hand to be spoken of, so called for that it borders upon the sea, for that this word *môr* in Welsh is the sea, and *morfa* is any land adjoining upon the sea shore; this quarter is the greatest & largest of the 4 & is good land.

Ricardston[9]

Ricardston being of late the mansion house of the Bowens of that place was as I find in ancient writings called Hoodstown of the Hoods the first owner thereof, for this was the ancient inheritance of Lucas de Hoda spoken of before . . . having lost the Bury & other lands was forced to take this Ricardston and Jordanston being a village next adjoining his mansion place, which Lucas de Hoda had issue two sons Ricard and Jordan who parting their father's patrimony between them called each part after their own names, Ricard de Hoda calling his part Ricardston and Jordan Jordanston which names continue to this day. Ricardston continued in the name of Hood until it descended unto one Perkin Hood . . . This Perkin had issue Llywelyn father to Griffith . . .

having but one daughter   married a gentleman of Cardiganshire called David ab Owen ap Meredith of Cwrrws in Iscoed whose daughter and coheir Dyddgu married Mathias ab Owen third brother to Sir James Bowen of Pentre Ifan knight whose son Owen ap Mathias ab Owen was father to Morgan father to Rhys[10] whose issue being extinct the inheritance fell to his 4 sisters Agnes wife of John Owen Phillips esquire, Alison wife of William Owen, Margaret wife of John Philip Young & Katherine Morgan between which sisters and their heirs at this instant there is no small trouble for the quartering of this house & demesne and great sums of money already spent. The arms of the Bowens of this house is that of Pentre Ifan with the difference of a third brother and that of Lucas de Hoda.[11]

Tregaman

Tregaman, in English Caman's town, takes the name of the river Caman that springs and passes through the townred & was called as I find it written in old evidence *Blaen Caman*, that is the point or spring of the Caman. This was the ancient inheritance of the Peverells,[12] gentlemen of sort in ancient time descended of Peverell of the knights that came to the conquest of Cemais with Martin de Tours & had this and diverse other lands given him by his lord where his issue continued & in the time of Henry VI that it came to one John Peverell who parted this and other his inheritance between his three sons, Howell, Jenkin & Owen. Of the issue of this Owen I have said before in Bayvil. The eldest son Howell had issue 2 daughters, Anne who died issueless & Eva who married Rhys Morgan of Cardiganshire who also had 2 daughters, Nest wife of John Cole, and Morfydd wife to William Thomas Philpin. John Cole had issue Howell Cole father to David Cole & James Cole. William Thomas Philpin had issue Phillip Thomas Philpin and William Thomas Philpin. The second son of Jenkin Peverell had issue Ievan father to Howell father to Howell Junior father to William Powell Peverell father to Thomas William Powell Peverell father to John who sold his patrimony as did Esau. And Ievan Thomas William yet living poorly. The Coles and Philpins aforesaid sold the whole townred of Tregaman to Thomas Peter father to Sage his daughter & coheir wife to Thomas Phillip Young who now enjoys the same & lately has built a new house upon the same. For the coats of the Youngs see after in Glastir.

Glastir[13]

Glastir the inheritance of Thomas Mathias took the name of the fertility & fair hue of the soil & signifies in English Greenfield for of all other places of the county it shows itself greenest in the spring and summer. It was in times past the parsonage house or glebe of the parson of Nevern before the appropriating thereof to the College of Saint David's as before I have declared in 'Nevern', and taking from this house the Park or Close called yet Parc y Clastir and bestowing it as the 4th part of the glebe as he did of all the rest of the fruits, upon the vicar, left the house & the other 3 parts of the lands to the said College, where it continued until the suppressing thereof when it was taken into the King's hands & bought by Mathias Thomas father to the said Thomas Mathias.[14]

And for that the said Thomas Mathias is the chief of the family of Youngs as heir of the eldest brother I will here speak of the said family for avoiding of prolixity & that I may in other places refer their original to this place. The said Youngs is an ancient family and are descended of the Coles and give the same coat. The ancient seat was Tredrysi of which I shall speak of next & after many of that name at last that descended from one Howell ap Jenkin Young with whom I will begin, for there the family began to spread. This Howell had issue by Margaret Mathew a woman of Anglesey five sons all tall men and well matched & of whom all of the name & many other are descended but as is affirmed all born before marriage, their names were Lewis Young, David Young, Howell Young, Guto Young & Thomas Young.

Lewis Young the eldest son married Gwenllian Voel of Colston a gentlewoman & heir of diverse lands who had issue Thomas Lewis father to Mathias Thomas father to Thomas Mathias so that notwithstanding that they have forgone the name of Young yet is he chief of the family.

David Young second son married Jane daughter of Sir James Bowen knight & had issue Richard who had Alice daughter & sole heir wife to Rees Morgan gentleman of Moylgrove son & heir to Morgan Jones lord of Towyn who enjoys her inheritance.

Howell Young married Gwenllian daughter of Rees Powell Fawr of Cardiganshire a gentleman well descended who had by her William Young of Nevern who selling his patrimony to Thomas George Bowen left behind him one daughter who lives in poor estate. He had also Rees ap Howell Young father to William Prys Young father to David now living.

Guto Young the fourth brother had 3 sons of whom there is in the county many issues but of mean estate.

Tredrysi

Thomas Young the youngest brother married Margaret the daughter of Howell Picton by whom he had issue Phillip who was father to Rowland Young of Tredrysi, John Phillip Young of Crugiau & Thomas Phillip Young of Tregaman & diverse others. This Thomas Young bought Tredrysi being his father's seat & inheritance, for after the birth of these five sons, the said Howell ap Jenkin Young married the said Margaret Mathew and has issue only one daughter named Elen wife to David ab Ievan David whose son named Rhydderch sold Tredrysi to this Thomas Young the youngest of the five brothers whose issue now enjoy it. This Tredrysi in English signifies Brambleton.

The coat of the Youngs & Coles is *vert* a hart tripping gardant between three fleur-de-lis *or*.[15]

This family of the Youngs were in times past noted to be men tall of person, fair of complexion and gentle of behaviour, but now some decline from the same.

Trellyffant[16]

Trellyffant is the mansion house of Owen Picton as it has been to 3 or 4 of his ancestors before, but in ancient time the land of Howell ap Jenkin of Nevern. It is in English & not unworthily called Toadstown for this is the place spoken of by Giraldus Cambrensis of a man consumed and eaten up with toads in miraculous sort. He delivers the story in this sort: I will not pass in silence (says he) two accidents that befell in this country of Cemais, the one in our time, the other not long before, & therefore that happened in our days, was that a young man born in these parts lying sick a-bed was so molested with toads that all the toads of the country gathered upon him as it were by appointment, & when they were killed by his attendants and friends the multitude increased liked Hydra's heads flocking to him from everywhere. At last when all his friends and others his neighbours were tired herewith, the young man was laid on top of a high tree that they had its boughs lopped off, where notwithstanding he was not in safety from these his poisoned enemies, for they climbed up the tree thick and threefold and devoured him to the very bones, that he died miserably. His name was Seisyll Esgair Hir, that is Longshanks. The coat of the Pictons is *gules* three pikes naiant *argent*.

Nevern Castle

Nevern Castle now utterly defaced yet does the site thereof show of what strength it was in times past being sited on a high hill inaccessible on the one part & strengthened with a mighty ditch hewn out of the main rock of the other part. This was the chief house of the Lords of Cemais in the time of the Lord Rhys, and this is the same castle wherein the same valiant Lord Rhys ap Gruffydd, prince of Wales, was imprisoned when he was taken prisoner by his sons: and this is that same castle called Castle Lanhyfer, the chief castle of Cemais, for which the said Lord Rhys broke his faith & promise with his son-in-law William Martin spoken of by the said Giraldus[17] in his journey through Cemais, wherein I cannot ever pass the mistaking of Doctor Powell in his annotations upon that place of Giraldus where he says that this castle called by Giraldus Cambrensis *In principal de Kemes Castro scilicet apud Lanhyuer* says this as Newport Castle, where indeed there was then the castle of Llanhyfer then standing & since by the said Sir William Martin was the castle and town of Newport being built, which castle of Llanhyfer being since utterly defaced and raised is known but of few & therefore by some that knew not the place informed Mr Powell that the Castle of Newport now being the chief castle of Cemais & standing also upon the river of Nevern was that wherein the great Lord Rhys was imprisoned by his sons.

Trewern

Trewern is the next quarter that comes to be spoken being the first part of south Nevern and is enclosed with the river Nevern on the north, both Clydachs on the east and west sides and parted by Cilgwyn most by land meres. This quarter always shows a leap year when it

Trewern Arms with arms of Gwynfardd Dyfed on sign.

comes to vicar's part. It takes the name of Trewern, the mansion house of William Warren esquire being in that quarter.

Pentre Ifan[18]

Pentre Ifan being the chief house & place not only of this quarter but of this county as that which is most ancient of gentry of all others and which has continued longest of account & in reputation of any in this part of Wales, & out of which there is more houses and branches sprung forth than I can reckon of any other in all the county, for herehence as from the chief head & spring does arise many houses & persons to be spoken of, as also some already treated of. I will as well for the ease of myself as of the readers take more pains in this place to ease myself & them in many other places, and as touching the original descents our ancient books of Genealogies begin at [*Lliw*] *Hen*, *Tywysog Prydain*, that is in English a Duke of Great Britain, who had a son called Pŷr y Dwyrain, that is Pirrhus of the East, who had a son called Gwynfardd Dyfed, that is, the happy bard of Demetia, whose son was Cuhelyn Fardd, of whom the ancient genealogies report many & strange things. This Cuhelyn had a son called Gwrwared ap

95

Cuhelyn. All this before written is authorised only by the Welsh books of genealogy for other matter did I never see or read of, but that this Cuhelyn had the forenamed Gwrwared and one Llywelyn to his sons is proved by an ancient deed made by the Lord Nicholas Martin, Lord of Cemais, to the said Gwrwared & Llywelyn, sons of Cuhelyn of the mountain of Presely which deed is without date. This Gwrwared ap Cuhelyn had a son Gwilym ap Gwrwared who had Gwrwared who married Gwenllian, daughter of Ednyfed Fychan & had issue Gwilym which by 3 several wives had issue six sons, namely two by each of them, of whom one called Eynon father to Owen father to Llywelyn father to Ievan father to William father to Owen father to Sir James ab Owen knight father to Owen ab Owen esquire, a second son, father to Thomas ab Owen esquire father to Elizabeth his daughter & coheir who now enjoys the house & was first married to Lewis Phillips gentleman son & heir to Eynon Phillips esquire by whom she has many children & is now married to Rees Lloyd gentleman by whom she has also issue. The wood of Cilrhydd adjoins to this house being a fair wood & best timber of this shire & is parcel & chief part of the demesnes, that is almost a wonder to see so fair timber to . . .[19]

Pentre Ifan gatehouse.

Trewern

Trewern, the mansion house of William Warren esquire, so called for it stands in a moor or marsh ground & might well be Englished Orleton or Moorton, for *wern* in Welsh signifies a marshy ground, or moor where orles do grow, or the orle tree itself. I find it called in ancient writing Trewern Waelod. It is the ancient inheritance of the said William Warren for diverse hundred years past, how ancient, it is not well known, & member of Pentre Ifan, for Warren David Voel whereof first they began to take the name of Warren, was son to David Voel ap David ab Owen ab Eynon ap Gwrwared ap Gwilym afore mentioned in Pentre Ifan, which Owen ab Eynon is said to marry the daughter of Sir William Cantington knight whose mother was the daughter of the Lord Rhys. The forenamed Warren David Voel had issue Ievan ap Warren, father to Lewis Warren father to William Warren father to Lewis Warren father to John Warren father to William Warren father to Mathias Warren father to the now William Warren, his wife is Jane one of the daughters & coheirs of Thomas ab Owen of Pentre Ifan esquire, his mother was a Catharne & hers the sister of Sir James William knight. The wife of William Warren was Janet natural daughter to Sir Rhys ap Thomas knight.[20]

The said William Warren may bear the two coats of Pentre Ifan before mentioned in Pentre Ifan as paternally descended from Gwrwared ap Gwilym. I have also seen written in ancient hand another coat allowed for the Warrens which was thus blazed . . .[21]

Llystyn[22]

Llystyn signifies in English a full court or palace, a house now altogether ruinated & used as a dairy in times past being of great account for this was the mansion house & portion of Rhys Llywelyn ab Owen, one of the five sons of Llywelyn ab Owen aforenamed, for we find written thus that Llywelyn ab Owen had five sons & five daughters & that Rhys Llywelyn ab Owen had this place called Llystyn. Ievan Llywelyn ab Owen had Pentre Ifan, Philip Llywelyn ab Owen had Panteg in Velfrey & Owen Fychan Llywelyn ab Owen had Argoed. This Rhys Llywelyn ab Owen has also five sons & as many daughters as shall be declared hereafter. Gwilym ap Rhys his eldest son had this house who was first and chief ancestor of the family of

Trewern.

the Gwilyms of this place, & had issue Rhys Gwilym & many other. This Rhys was father to Ellyw his sole heir, wife to Harry Bowen of Lochmeyler father to Richard Bowen, who also had Richard father to Katherine Bowen now wife of John Scourfield esquire, but some of the ancestors of the said Katherine growing to unthriftiness did away the house & the demesnes to Owen ab Owen of Pentre Ifan esquire father to Thomas Bowen after whose death it fell to the part of Jane Bowen youngest daughter & coheir to the said Thomas Bowen & wife to the said William Warren who now in her right enjoys the same as a grange or dairy adjoining Trewern. I remember in my time a fair grove of trees about the house which now is rotted & the land tilled. Out of this house of Llystyn (as is partly touched before & shall be more hereafter) is sprung forth diverse houses of gentlemen.

Argoed

Argoed took the name of the situation thereof having sometimes a forest of wood under it called Coed Cadw,[23] for Argoed is in English over or above the wood, which wood of Coed Cadw is now utterly consumed. The mansion house of John Bowen Fychan gentleman being a house of long continuance for as I said last, this & much other land was the portion of Owen Fychan son to Llywelyn ab Owen, who had issue Howel ab Owen Fychan which Howel had two sons, Thomas & Llywelyn, between whom he parted his inheritance giving Argoed & diverse lands with the same to Thomas, and to Llywelyn he gave Trecoeged & diverse other tenements near hand. Thomas of Argoed had issue James Thomas ap Howel, father to Rhys Griffith and Mathias. Rhys sold Argoed to Mathias his younger brother who by his will devised the same to John Bowen Fychan who now enjoys it. Llywelyn the other son of the said Howel ab Owen who had Trecoeged had issue John Llywelyn ap Howel who having but one son named William John & that illegitimate, entailed this & other his lands to him in tail special the remainder to William Owen of Henllys esquire & his heirs in fee, which William John the son dying issueless, the right descended to the said William Owen whose son & heir George Owen about five years past recovered the same.

The arms of the said John Bowen Fychan are those of Pentre Ifan with the difference of a fourth brother descended of a third. The arms of the issue of the said Owen Fychan is also that of Pentre Ifan.

Llwyngwair

Llwyngwair, the mansion house of James Bowen gentleman in English signifies the hay grove,[24] the house & demesnes more than half compassed with the river of Nevern yielding as well commodity of fishing as other pleasures. The seat pleasant for wood & water, it was in former time the original seat of the Coles & by some of them sold to Sir James Bowen & his lady, Mary Herle, & by them assured to their son Mathias Bowen father to this James Bowen where he now inhabits. The mother of the said James Bowen was of the Philipps, her mother a Dyer & hers a Bontan. The mother of Mathias Bowen was Herle & hers the sister of Sir Rhys ap Thomas knight. He bears the coat of Pentre Ifan with the difference of a third brother.

Cole

Cole's coat is *vert* a hart tripping between three fleur-de-lis *or*. It is said that Cole of Llwyngwair[25] was the first that found out marl in Cemais for mending the land & that he learned the same in France &

brought from thence an auger to find it out & that the first marl land of all this county was at Llwyngwair.

Nevern villa

The townred of Nevern being some time a borough & having a portreeve & courts belonging to it is now decayed & become rural and the privileges discontinued. It consisted of 18 burgages & takes the name of the river Nevern that passes by the town.

Howel ap Jenkin

Here was the mansion house of Howel ap Jenkin ap Robert the Younger, the greatest man of living in his time in all the county & now his heirs grown to that poverty that they are scarce known who they are if any be living. The said Howel ap Jenkin the younger built there a fair house but died before the same was finished. He married daughter of Sir [William] Perrot knight & by her had issue a son named William who consumed the whole inheritance,[26] and it is said that Howel ap Jenkin the father being a learned man died at the birth of his son William cast at his nativity whereby he presently told his wife that she had borne a son that should consume & spend all that he & his ancestors had gathered; and thereupon as it is reported the said Howel ap Jenkin determining to prevent fate made some estate of his lands, such as he thought that his son might not sell the same, & did especially repose trust in one Morgan Taylor, a mean & base fellow maintained by his alms & was parish clerk & wholly fed & relieved by the said Howel ap Jenkin & therefore as much tied to the said Howel ap Jenkin as that he thought none might be better trusted than he. After the death of the said Howel ap Jenkin his son William fulfilled his foreseen fortune & left not one foot of land unsold & the said Morgan Taylor turning his trust to treachery joined with his master's unthrifty heir in all sales & therefore there is many feoffments yet extant wherein William ap Howel ap Jenkin & Morgan Taylor do join in sale of the land & this makes many to muse at this day to see these feoffments made by them both yet well known to be Howel ap Jenkin's land, this being the only cause so that to prevent the determined will of God no wordly policy can prevail, and who so trusts base minded people shall be served of them in their kind. The

100

arms of the said Howel ap Jenkin was that of Pentre Ifan being paternally descended from thence.

Maen y gromlech[27]

Maen y gromlech, a huge stone mounted on high upon three others stands east of Cilrhydd wood upon the land of Pentre Ifan of whose rare & strange erecting I have spoken of in my former book among the wonders of this shire.

Cilgwyn

Cilgwyn, the fourth & last quarter of the parish of Nevern is the most southerly part there having been in it much mountains & hills & many rivers and brooks rising in the same & is more apt for breeding of cattle than for corn. The river Gwaun spoken of in my first book has her rising here, so has also Syfynwy & east & west Clydachs. It has in it the hamlet of Tregynon which is between the brooks of Cuad & Lygen, Esgair Gynon between Gwaun & Lygen, Pencelli Fawr, Llawr y Cilgwyn & Pennant-ddu. It has in it the chapel of Cilgwyn, being a chapel of ease dedicated to the Virgin Mary & consecrated within the memory of men now living, where they have divine service & *Jura parochialia* to the full [y]et parishioners undergoing all charges with their mother church of Nevern.

Ffynnon Brynach

Ffynnon Brynach, the well of Brynach, whereof Giraldus makes mention stands in this quarter above Cernydd Meibion Owen in the mountain by the highway's side, a pretty fine well compassed about with a curtilage of stone wall, which they call Buarth Brynach, Brynach's Fold, the wall being of 5 or 6 foot thick. Of this well Giraldus thus reports that a certain rich man dwelling on the north side of the Presely Hills, which must be near to this well standing within a quarter of a mile of the north side of Presely, dreamt said he 3 nights on row that if he would thrust his arm under a stone that covered the spring of this well, he should there find a chain of gold. The dreamer in hope of gain did so, where a serpent stung him in the thumb that he died thereof. This happened, said Giraldus, in the time of Henry the Second.

NOTES

NANHYFER / NEVERN

[1]Guest, Lady Charlotte, *The Mabinogion*, London, 1906, 131.

[2]Gerald of Wales, *The Journey through Wales / The Description of Wales*, ed. Lewis Thorpe, London, 1978, 170.

[3]*Archaeologia Cambrensis* 1922, 186.

[4]Dyfed Archaeological Trust Report 1991-2.

[5]*Inventory of Ancient Monuments in Wales and Monmouthshire: County of Pembroke*, HMSO, 1925, 761.

[6]Fenton, Richard, *A Historical Tour through Pembrokeshire*, London, 1903 (republ. 1994), 293.

[7]Owen, George, *The Description of Pembrokeshire*, ed. Dillwyn Miles, 1994, 194-5.

[8]Jones, Evan, in *The Pembrokeshire County Guardian*, 23 June 1900.

[9]Grimes, W F, *The Prehistory of Wales*, Cardiff, 1951, 176, 183.

[10]*Bulletin of the Board of Celtic Studies* ii (1925), 88.

[11]Rees, Siân, *A Guide to Ancient and Historic Wales: Pembrokeshire*, HMSO, 1992, 61-2.

[12]Boon, G E and Lewis, J M (eds.), *Welsh Antiquity*, Cardiff, 1976, 181.

[13]Jones, G Hartwell, *Celtic Britain and the Pilgrim Movement*, 1912, 371.

[14]*Inventory* 265.

SAINT BRYNACH

[1]Wade-Evans, A W, *Welsh Christian Origins*, Oxford, 1934, 151.

[2]Evans, J T, *The Church Plate of Pembrokeshire*, London, 1905, 68.

[3]Bartrum, P C, *A Welsh Classical Dictionary*, National Library of Wales, 1993, 68.

[4]Henken, Elissa R, *Traditions of Welsh Saints*, Bury St Edmunds, 1987, 277.

[5]Wade-Evans, 152.

[6]Bartrum, 131.

[7]*ibid.*, 67.

[8]Wade-Evans, 153.

[9]Bartrum, 440.

[10]Fenton, 542n.

[11]Jones, Francis, *The Holy Wells of Wales*, Cardiff, 1954, 203.

[12]Fenton, 195.

[13]Jones, Francis, 1954, 39.

[14]Bowen, E G, *The Settlements of the Celtic Saints in Wales*, Cardiff, 1956, 28.

[15]Bartrum, 64-5.

NEVERN CASTLE

[1]Miles, Dillwyn, *The Ancient Borough of Newport in Pembrokeshire*, Haverfordwest, 1995, 12.

[2]Gruffydd, R G, 'A Poem in Praise of Cuhelyn Fardd from the Black Book of Carmarthen' in *Studia Celtica*, X/XI (1975-76), 198-200.

[3]Gerald of Wales, 171.

[4]King, D J C, *Castellum Anglicanum*, New York, 1983, 402.

[5]Williams, J (Ab Ithel) (ed.), *Annales Cambriae*, London, 1860, 60.

[6]King, 1983, 395.

[7]Rees, William, *A History of the Order of St John of Jerusalem in Wales*, Cardiff, 1947, 28.

[8]King, D J C, *pers. comm.* and in *Arch. Camb.*, 1951, 123-8.

[9]Turvey, Roger, 'Nevern Castle: A New Interpretation' in *The Journal of the Pembrokeshire Historical Society*, 3 (1989), 58.

NEVERN CHURCHYARD

[1]Mitchell, Alan, *pers. comm.* 18. 5. 1993.

[2]Patch, Derek, Arboricultural Advisory and Information Service, *pers. comm.* 6. 7. 1993.

[3]Wilks, J H, *Trees of the British Isles in History and Legend*, 88.

[4]Gregory, D, *Country Churchyards in Wales*, Llanrwst, 1991, 40-2.

[5]Lewis, Samuel, *A Topographical Dictionary of Wales*, London, 1848, 258.

[6]*Arch. Camb.*, 1896, 290.

[7]Nash-Williams, V E, *The Early Christian Monuments of Wales*, Cardiff, 1950, 197.

[8]Bartrum, 325.

[9]Nash-Williams, 197.

NEVERN CHURCH

[1]Lewis, Samuel, 258.

[2]*Arch. Camb.*, 1922, 501.

[3]*ibid.*, 501.

[4]Jones, Francis, 'Philipps of Pentre Ifan', *penes me*.

[5]Camden, William, *Britannia*, ed. E Gibson, London, 1722, 762-3.

[6]*Arch. Camb.*, 1986, 134.

[7]Nash-Williams, 197.

[8]*Arch. Camb.*, 1922, 501.

[9]*ibid.*, 1905, 167.

[10]*ibid.*, 1922, 500.

[11]Nash-Williams, 197.

[12]*Arch. Camb.*, 1922, 501.

[13]*ibid.*, 500.

[14]*The Church of St Brynach, Nevern, Pembrokeshire* (Guidebook), Appendix B, 16.

[15]Evans, J T, 1905, 68.

[16]Charles, B G, 'The Vicarage and Tithes of Nevern in Pembrokeshire' in the *Journal of the Historical Society of the Church in Wales* I, 2 (1947), 26.

[17]*ibid.*, 28.

[18]*ibid.*, 31.

[19]Green, F and Barker, T, 'Pembrokeshire Parsons' in *West Wales Historical Records* III, Carmarthen, 1913, 217.

[20]Charles, B G, 1947, 29-30.

[21]Green and Barker, III, 218-9.

[22]Charles, B G, 1947, 31-2.

[23]Charles, B G, 'The Second Book of George Owen's Description of Penbrokshire' in the *National Library of Wales Journal*, V, 4 (1948) 271.

[24]Charles, 1947, 37n.

[25]*ibid.*, 33.

[26]Green and Barker, II, 230.

[27]Charles, 1947, 37.

[28]Green and Barker, III, 218-9.

[29]*Arch. Camb.*, 1935, 302.

[30]Green and Barker, III, 218-9.

[31]Owen, George, *The Description of Penbrokshire*, ed. Henry Owen, II (1897), 509.

NONCONFORMISM

[1]Jones, Anthony, *Welsh Chapels*, National Museum of Wales, 1996, 8.

[2]*ibid.*, 12.

[3]*ibid.*, 4.

[4]Lewis, D Morgan, *Cofiant y Diweddar Barchedig Evan Lewis, Brynberian*, Aberystwyth, 1903, 111.

[5]Rees and Thomas, *Hanes Eglwysi Annibynnol Cymru*, Dolgellau, 1891, 39.

[6]Lewis, D Morgan, 117.

[7]*ibid.*, 222.

[8]Morris, Caleb, *Braslun o Hanes Eglwys Ebeneser, Trefdraet*h, Aberdâr, 1944, 10.

[9]Thomas, B B, 'James Davies (Siams Dafydd) 1758-1844' in the *National Library of Wales Journal*, XVIII, 1, 1973, 56.

[10]Miles, Dillwyn, 1995, 96-9.

[11]Williams, A H (ed.), *John Wesley in Wales*, Cardiff, 1971, 66.

[12]Roberts, Gomer M, *Y Pêr Ganiedydd* I, (1949), 149.

[13]*ibid.*, 211.

[14]*ibid.*, II, 82.

[15]Owen, J Morgan, *Capel Gethsemane (MC) Morfa, ger Trefdraeth, 1944*.
[16]Jones, T R, *Penuel Cemaes 1824-1976*.

NEVERN SCHOOL

[1]*The Dictionary of Welsh Biography down to 1940*, London, 1959, 430.
[2]*ibid.*, 34.
[3]*Report of the Commissioners of Enquiry into the State of Education in Wales under R R W Lingen*, HMSO, 1847.
[4]Lewis, D Morgan, 224-6.

NEVERN PARISH COUNCIL

[1]Arnold-Baker, Charles, *Local Government Administration*, London, 1981, 3-4.

NEVERN NOTABLES

[1]Jones, Francis, 'Bowen of Pentre Ifan and Llwyngwair' in *The Pembrokeshire Historian*, 6 (1979), 37-9.
[2]*ibid.*, 45-6.
[3]Miles, Dillwyn, 1995, 96.
[4]Jones, Francis, 1979, 53-4.
[5]Jones, Evan, 'Reverend David Griffiths, Vicar of Nevern' in *The Pembrokeshire County Guardian*, 19 January 1901.
[6]Baker-Jones, D L, 'The Letters of the Reverend David Griffiths, Nevern, 1756-1834' in the *National Library of Wales Journal*, XX, 2, 1977, 169-176.
[7]Jones, Evan, 26 January 1901.
[8]Jones, Francis, 1979, 53.
[9]Miles, Dillwyn, 1995, 115.
[10]Baker-Jones, 176.
[11]*The Dictionary of Welsh Biography down to 1940*, London, 1959, 386.
[12]*ibid.*, 430-1.
[13]Miles, Dillwyn, *The Royal National Eisteddfod of Wales*, Swansea, 1978, 33.
[14]Howell, J, *Blodau Dyfed*, Carmarthen, 1824, 359.
[15]*ibid.*, 214.
[16]Lloyd, D & M (ed), *A Book of Wales*, London, 1953, 114.
[17]*The Dictionary of Welsh Biography down to 1940*, London, 1959, 478.
[18]Green, F & Barker, T, 'Pembrokeshire Parsons' in *West Wales Historical Records*, V, 219.
[19]Jones, T Gwynn, *Llawlyfr Llenyddiaeth Gymraeg yn y Ddeunawfed Ganrif*, 1920, 15.
[20]Stephens, M (ed), *The Oxford Companion to the Literature of Wales*, Oxford, 1986, 311.

[21]Miles, Dillwyn, *The Secret of the Bards of the Isle of Britain*, Dinefwr Press, 1992, 85ff.

[22]Bessborough, The Earl of, *The Diaries of Lady Charlotte Guest*, London, 1950, 66ff.

[23]Guest, Revel & John, Angela, *Lady Charlotte Guest: A Biography of the Nineteenth Century*, 1989, 113.

[24]Carr, Glenda, *William Owen Pughe*, Caerdydd, 1983, 207.

[25]*The County Echo*, Fishguard, 8 May 1952.

[26]McDonald, R W, 'Cofrestri Plwyf Cymru' in *The National Library of Wales Journal*, XIX, 2 (1975), 128-130.

[27]*The Dictionary of Welsh Biography down to 1940*, 579.

[28]*Yr Haul*, XVII (Awst 1915), 198.

[29]Jones, Francis, 'Lloyd of Hendre and Cwmgloyn' in *The National Library of Wales Journal*, XXIII, 4 (1984), 345-7.

[30]*The Dictionary of Welsh Biography down to 1940*, 595

[31]*ibid.*, 1142-3.

[32]Charles, B G, *George Owen of Henllys: A Welsh Elizabethan*, Aberystwyth, 1973.

[33]Owen, George, *The Description of Pembrokeshire*, ed. Dillwyn Miles, Gomer Press, 1994, xxxvii.

[34]*The Dictionary of Welsh Biography down to 1940*, 723.

[35]Evans, Penry, *pers. comm.*

NEVERN 1600

[1]The patronage passed from the lords of Cemais to the College of St Mary at St David's in 1377.

[2]Henllys means 'old court' or 'old hall' and the name was probably taken from the promontory fort Castell Henllys. It was the largest house in the parish and was shown as having ten hearths in the Hearth Tax returns for 1670. Llwyngwair had six hearths and Trewern and Cwmgloyn had five each.

[3]George Owen resorted to 'creative genealogy' in an effort to 'prove' that his father had obtained the lordship of Cemais by inheritance rather than by purchase. His claim to be descended from Llywelyn ap Rhydderch cannot be sustained, and Richard de Hoda would have had to wait a century before he could have married Alice Martin who, if she ever existed, could not have been heiress to the lordship.

[4]In the pedigree that Owen gave Lewys Dwnn in 1591, Anne is described as 'Ancred daughter of William Obiled of Carmarthen, gent.' Her father also appears as Gwilym Abolet and was described as a warden of the corporation of tuckers in Carmarthen, whose wife was Elizabeth Griffith of Tenby.

[5]Cwmgloyn, 'the valley of the Gloyn', where *gloyn* may refer to the 'clear' or 'bright' water of the river. Fenton observed that Cwmgloyn was 'the only

mansion of the many in its neighbourhood which is not in ruins or has been metamorphosed into a farmhouse.' It originally comprised three sides of a square, but the east wing was demolished. It has a Jacobean staircase and it is claimed that an ogham stone is hidden behind the plaster in one of the rooms. A gargoylish carved head decorates one of the entrance gate piers, while another, on the other side, has disappeared.

Thomas Lloyd, the last of the Lloyds, was an improving landlord and farmer and the owner of three coastal vessels (see pp. 74, 80).

The farm was occupied in 1940 by the naturalist R M Lockley when he had to vacate the island of Skokholm, and it was the subject of his book *Inland Farm*.

[6]William Griffith's son, George William Griffith, born in 1584, was 'servant in livery' to George Owen of Henllys and was one his most able amanuenses. He became a recognised genealogist and it was largely through him that much of George Owen's genealogical learning was passed on to later generations. He married Maud Bowen of Llwyngwair and, at his father's death, he settled down on his patrimony at Penybenglog. Penybenglog was later the home of the Reverend Watkin Lewes, rector of Meline, whose son, Sir Watkin Lewes, was the first Pembrokeshire man to be Lord Mayor of London.

[7]Glanduad, 'the bank of the river Duad', where *duad* may refer to the 'dark' bed of the stream.

[8]Llwyngores: the name is derived from *llwyn*, a tree or grove, and *gores(t)*, open, unenclosed or waste land.

[9]Ricardston, the farm or homestead of Richard (de Hoda): the Welsh Trericard has become Treicert. The de Hoda or Hood family were tenants of the Martins in Rattery in Devon. There is no account of Richard but his brother, Jordan, whose patrimony was nearby Trefwrdan or Jordanston, witnessed a number of deeds in Cemais between 1240 and 1278.

[10]Rhys ap Morgan ab Owen held Treicert by payment of 'a red rose annually upon the Feast of Saint John the Baptist *super lapidem vocatur Leghtrivett*.

[11]George Owen claimed that the coat of arms of Lucas de Hoda was *gules* a boar *argent* armed gristled collared and chained *or* chained to a holly bush, which he also registered as his own coat. There is no evidence that Hood bore such a coat.

[12]Robert FitzMartin married Matilda, or Maud, the widow of William Peverel who is given as of Tregaman, and alternatively of Tregamon near Bodmin. Some time before 1121 Robert and Matilda gave the land of William Peverel at Vengeons, in La Manche, to the abbey of Savigny.

Nicholas FitzMartin married as his second wife Isabel, widow of Hugh Peverel of Ermington whose son, Sir John Peverel, obtained a lease of

Newport castle for his life in exchange for his manor of Kingston in Devon. Sir John presented the living of Ermington to his half-brother, David Martin, later Bishop of St David's.

[13]Glastir derives from the Welsh *clas*, a monastic community, and *tir*, land: the land of the monastic community or glebe land. The Papal Register of 1444 referred to 'the glebe or lands of the said parish church of Neverne commonly [called] Clastir in the barony of Kemmeys.'

[14]Thomas Mathias was the forebear of the Mathias families of Llangwaran and Lamphey Court.

[15]One member of the family, David Mathias, became a Moravian and changed his coat of arms to four dice cubes with eleven spots on each on a red shield, referring to the selection by lot of Matthias to replace Judas Iscariot: 'And they gave forth their lots: and the lot fell upon Matthias, and he was numbered with the eleven apostles.' (Acts 1, 26).

[16]The name first appears as Trellyffan or Trellyffain and could consist of *tref*, homestead, and *llyffant*, a toad: the final *t* is not pronounced locally, and the plural would be *llyffantod* rather than *llyffaint*. It could also derive from the personal name Llyffan. Siôn Dafydd Rhys (*c*1600) stated that a giant called Llyffan Gawr lived at Castell Llyffan Gawr in the parish of Llanfair Orllwyn in Cardiganshire. Dinas Island was formerly known as Ynys Fach Llyffan Gawr.

Giraldus's onomastic tale persisted in the family as a crest on rings and teaspoons. A figure of a toad, in dark green-veined marble, was built into the parlour chimney-piece at Trellyffan, sent from Italy by Sir Richard Mason, Knight of the Green Cloth to James II. It was later removed and shown among a collection of objects of interest assembled at Cardigan during the visit of the Cambrian Archaeological Association in 1859 (along with the wig that Oliver Cromwell had left at Trellyffant!). The toad, and the wig, had been provided by Grace Owen, wife of Morris Williams Lloyd Owen who had inherited Trellyffan from his father, Owen Owen of Cwmgloyn, and had by then moved to Kent House, Haverfordwest.

In 1975 Colonel Hugh Higgon, formerly Lord Lieutenant, who was the executor of Mrs Owen's will, informed the author that Morris Owen 'had led a riotous life and lost all his money—at the Ludlow Races.' He used to visit Kent House when he was a boy and remembered seeing the Trellyffan Toad there, but it had disappeared by the time he was executor.

[17]Giraldus was a nephew of The Lord Rhys but that did not prevent him being strong in his condemnation of the treatment of William FitzMartin.

[18]Pentre Ifan is first mentioned as the inheritance of Ievan ab Owen, the second son of Owen ap Robert ap Gwrwared, in a deed of 1342. Ievan died without issue and Pentre Ifan passed to his nephew, Evan ap Llywelyn ab Owen o'r Coed. 'Coed' referred to Coed Cilrhydd, the wood that surrounded

Pentre Ifan and it may have been the old name for the house. Evan, who was steward of Pembroke in 1413, built a new house which became the chief seat of the Bowen family. A larger mansion house was probably built by his great-grandson, James ab Owen, who supported Henry Tudor on his march to Bosworth in 1485, and later received a knighthood for his services to the king. The gatehouse to the courtyard of this Tudor house has recently been renovated.

Sir James was appointed steward to Sir Walter Herbert, who was lord of Cemais following the attainder of Lord Audley in 1497, and he continued in that office when Audley's son was restored the barony. True to the tradition of his ancestors, he kept an open house for the itinerant bards, and eulogistic poems were addressed to him and to his wife by Ieuan Brechfa and Dafydd Nanmor.

By his first wife, Jane, daughter of Jenkin Perrot of Caerforiog, Sir James had four sons and five daughters. The eldest son having died without male issue, Owen Bowen, the second son, succeeded to Pentre Ifan on his father's death. He married Maud, daughter of Sir John Wogan of Wiston and was sheriff of the county of Pembroke in 1545. At his death, some five years later, he was followed at Pentre Ifan by his second son, Thomas Bowen who was a Justice of the Peace and sheriff in 1569. He married Anne, daughter of John Philipps of Picton Castle, by whom he had two daughters, Elizabeth and Jane. Jane married William Warren of Trewern, and Elizabeth, who had Pentre Ifan, married Lewis, son of Eynon Philipps of Cardigan Priory, and had issue.

[19]Left blank.

[20]The last of the Warrens died in 1757 leaving four daughters and coheiresses: Catherine, who married Philip Jones of Llanina; Jane, wife of Sir Basil Keith, Governor of Jamaica; Anne, who was the wife of Thomas Williams of Pope Hill, Haverfordwest, and Elizabeth, who married William Edwardes, created Baron Kensington, of the second creation, in 1776.

Trewern fell to the lot of Catherine who, at her death, passed it to her only son, Edward Warren Jones of Llanina. He died unmarried in 1829 and, by his will, he left all his property to Charlotte, daughter of Captain William Longcroft, RN, of Havant, Hants. Charlotte had married, in 1819, Thomas Lloyd of Coedmor, to whom Edward Jones was related through his grandmother, Elin Lloyd of Cilgwyn.

The house is Jacobean with a large porch which has a chamber above it. It was in this chamber that 'the Trewern Treasure' is alleged to have been found sometime around the middle of the nineteenth century. By then the house was occupied by a tenant farmer, David George, born at Glanllynan in the parish of Verwig, who had been ordained in 1838 to assist the Reverend William Owen, pastor of Caersalem Baptist Chapel, and later himself became the minister of that chapel and of Jabez Chapel in the Gwaun Valley. It is said that, following a storm, some slates had been removed from the roof of the chamber and that the mason engaged to replace them discovered that the chamber was sealed off from the rest of the house and that it contained a quantity of gold, believed to have been hidden during the Civil Wars. An embellished version stated that it was 'a golden image', pieces of which were hacked off by a blacksmith at his smithy, situated opposite Dolbont, and fashioned into nuggets which the farmer carried off to London to sell. Further refinements maintained that he developed a twitch of the head, gained by looking over his shoulder to see whether the devil was following him, and that the experience caused him to stutter, except when he preached or gave out a hymn.

David George, by 1875, was living at Brithdir Mawr, Newport, and the return of landowners for that year shows that he owned 362 acres of land from which he derived £235.12s.0d in rent. He was also the owner of Trenewydd, Ffynnonwen and Llystyn. He built Trefoel, to which his son, Thomas, moved from Henllys, and he also built Dyffryn Benglog. He was mayor of Newport in 1872-74. He died at Brithdir on 15 May 1892 and was buried at Caersalem.

[21]The 'two coats of Pentre Ifan' that William Warren bore were *azure*, a lion rampant in an orle of roses *or*, the arms attributed to Gwynfardd Dyfed, and *gules*, a chevron between three knots *argent*, the arms of Gwilym ab Owen o'r Coed which were said to have been awarded to him when he killed the king of France's champion called Tristram, whose arms were *gules* a chevron between three Tristram knots *argent*. The Tristram knot has four bows and is also known in heraldry as the Bowen knot, although it is claimed that it is so called in allusion to the name Bowen. The other coat that George Owen may have 'seen written' was probably *or*, two lions passant guardant *sable*, a fess vairy *or* and *azure* compony, which is given by Lewys Dwnn for Warren of Trewern.

[22]Llystyn derives from *llys* (court, hall) and *dynn* (a fortified enclosure). Llywelyn ap Gwilym of Llystyn, and of Dolgoch and Cryngae in Emlyn, was tutor and favourite uncle of Dafydd ap Gwilym who wrote fine poems in his praise, and a mournful elegy when he was murdered and his houses utterly destroyed—*A'r Llystyn yn arlloesty* (And Llystyn was a desolate place).

[23]Coedcadw was a term used in the Welsh laws for 'a preserved wood'.

[24]Llwyngwair probably means 'Gwair's grove': Gwair was the name of several legendary figures in the early Welsh tales and triads, including the fictitious Gwair of Caer Weir. It could also derive from *gwair* meaning a bend or a curve: as Owen said, the house is 'more than half encompassed with the river Nevern.'

Fenton maintained that Llwyngwair yielded 'to very few places in the county; being on the margin of a noble river, where the tide at spring is a little felt, encircled with majestic woods, with good gardens, and a highly cultivated demesne and commanding a pleasant view of the town of Newport and its castle, backed by the hoary mountain of Carningli.' The house is an amalgam of medieval, Tudor, Georgian and nineteenth century.

[25]Llwyngwair was said to have been granted to 'a french-man' named Cole, one of the Norman followers, and it remained in that family until the early part of the sixteenth century, though they left little evidence of their tenure. In 1308, John Cole was appointed by William Martin, lord of Cemais, to do suit for him at the court at Pembroke when he himself could not attend, and William Cole is named as a juror at Newport in 1326, and Richard Cole was granted a moiety of a burgage at Haverfordwest in 1459. In 1503 James Cole and David Cole released all claims to messuages and lands at Llwyngwair to Howel, son of Thomas Cole of Llwyngwair, and not long after that date Sir James ab Owen of Pentre Ifan puchased Llwyngwair and settled it upon Mathias Bowen, his eldest son by his second wife, Mary Herle.

[26]Howel ap Jenkin's profligate son, William, married Elen, daughter of Thomas ap Hywel ab Owen Fychan of Argoed by whom he had two sons, Owen, who was blind, and Lewis, both of whom died unmarried, and a daughter, Jane, who married secondly William James. Their son, Owen William, is believed to have sold the remainder of the Nevern estate to William Owen of Henllys. Fenton states that the ruins of Hywel's 'venerable old mansion' were still to be seen: the uneven surface of the field adjoining Court may give a clue to its location. The house was a favourite resort of the Welsh bards. Rhys Nanmor praises the warm reception he had received at 'the mansion by the river', and Lewis Glyn Cothi wrote a panegyrical ode to its generous host whom Hywel Swrdwal compared to a young salmon, and described as a leader of men, a scholar who knew four languages, an interpreter of the law and the defender of the weak throughout the lordship of Cemais. Whenever Swrdwal attended mass at Nevern church he hastened afterwards to Howel ap Jenkin's 'court to enjoy his wine and his hospitality.'

The arms of Howel ap Jenkin are usally given as *gules*, a chevron *argent* between in chief two fleur-de-lis and in base a lion rampant sinister *or*.

[27]George Owen had 'spoken of' Maen y gromlech in his *Description of Penbrokeshire* in which he provided the first known drawing of the Pentre Ifan cromlech. Fenton included an engraving by Sir Richard Colt Hoare in his *Historical Tour through Pembrokeshire*, and the cromlech was painted in oils by the great painter of megaliths, Richard Tongue of Bath in 1835.

INDEX